Chris,

Psalms 1:1-2

    Blessed is the man who does not get advice from ungodly people, instead he loves God's law and searches it with his heart all the time.

    We Love You
    Uncle Dave
      and
      Aunt Bridget.

PRESENTED TO

Chris

BY

Uncle Dave & Aunt Bridget

ON

July 17, 2011 :)

*"I am the good shepherd. I know my sheep, and they know me."*
(From Story 89)

# CLASSIC
# BIBLE
# STORYBOOK

BY KENNETH N. TAYLOR

ILLUSTRATIONS BY RICHARD AND FRANCES HOOK

Tyndale House Publishers, Inc. Carol Stream, Illinois

Visit Tyndale's exciting Web site for kids at www.tyndale.com/kids

*TYNDALE* and Tyndale's quill logo are registered trademarks of Tyndale House Publishers, Inc.

*Classic Bible Storybook*

Designed by Erik M. Peterson

Edited by Betty Free Swanberg

Adapted from *The Book for Children*, copyright © 2000 by Tyndale House Foundation, and *Taylor's Bible Story Book*, copyright © 1979 by Tyndale House Foundation. The material in *Taylor's Bible Story Book* is based on *The Story of the Bible*, written by Charles Foster.

**Library of Congress Cataloging-in-Publication Data**

Taylor, Kenneth Nathaniel.
 Classic Bible storybook / by Kenneth N. Taylor ; illustrations by Richard and Frances Hook.
   p. cm.
 ISBN-13: 978-1-4143-0769-5 (hc)
 ISBN-10: 1-4143-0769-1 (hc)
 1. Bible stories, English--Juvenile literature. I. Hook, Richard. II. Hook, Frances. III. Title.
 BS551.3.T36 2009
 220.9'505--dc22

                                                                         2008034385

Printed in China

15 14 13 12 11 10 09

7 6 5 4 3 2 1

# Contents

## NEW TESTAMENT

*Kenneth N. Taylor (1950) reading Bible stories to two of his children.*

# *Introducing the Author*

## Kenneth N. Taylor
## 1917–2005

Kenneth N. Taylor is best known as the writer of *The Living Bible*, a paraphrase he wrote so that his own children could better grasp Scripture's message. This paraphrase was later revised by a group of biblical scholars to become the New Living Translation.

It was always Dr. Taylor's desire to make Bible truths easily understandable to everyone—both adults and children. Ken Taylor's first claim to fame, though, was as a writer of children's books. Ken and his wife, Margaret, had ten children and twenty-eight grandchildren. (The number of great-grandchildren continues to grow!) So Ken Taylor personally told many children about God. His early manuscripts were ready for publication only when they passed the scrutiny of his ten young critics!

Dr. Taylor's children's books, which have been read to three generations of children around the world, include *The Bible in Pictures for Little Eyes* (Moody Press), *Devotions for the Children's Hour* (Moody Press), *Taylor's Bible Story Book* (Tyndale House), *The Living Bible Story Book* (Tyndale House), and *Big Thoughts for Little People* (Tyndale House). Some of his more recent books include *My First Bible in Pictures* (Tyndale House), *I Can Learn about God* (Tyndale House), *A Child's First Bible* (Tyndale House), *The Book for Children* (Tyndale House), and *Family-Time Bible in Pictures* (Tyndale House).

Dr. Taylor believed that it was important for the illustrations in his books to make the words come to life. Just as the words were to be easy for children to understand, so were the illustrations. He especially appreciated Richard and Frances Hook for their realistic, accurate portrayal of biblical scenes along with sweet pictures of children. Their illustrations, along with Dr. Taylor's stories, can easily form the basis for many lively family discussions about the Bible.

*Adam and Eve lived in the beautiful garden God made.*

# God Makes a Beautiful World

GENESIS 1-2; 3:20

Long, long ago—before anyone can remember—God made the world. At first it was lonely and dark.

Then God made the light. He said, "Let there be light," and light came. God was pleased with it. He called the light "day." And he called the darkness "night." God did these things on the first day of Creation.

Then God made the space above the earth. He called it "sky." God did this on the second day of Creation.

Next God said that the waters covering the earth should become oceans and lakes, and dry land should appear. God also made grass grow, and bushes and trees. All this was on the third day of Creation.

On the fourth day God let the sun shine in the daytime, and the moon and stars at night.

On the fifth day God made large sea animals and little fish. And he made birds, like ducks and geese, to fly over the water and swim in it. He made other birds, like eagles, robins, pigeons, and wrens, to fly over the land and live in the woods and fields.

On the sixth day of Creation God made animals that walk on land. He made wild elephants, lions, tigers, and bears. He made tame rabbits, horses, cows, and sheep. And he made little insects, such as ants and bees.

Then God made someone very special. He took some dust from the ground and formed it into a man's body. God gave life to the body, and the man began to breathe. God named the man Adam.

The Lord God planted the beautiful Garden of Eden as a home for Adam. In it God planted trees full of delicious fruit. God told Adam he could eat any fruit except the fruit from one tree. That was the tree of the knowledge of good and evil. If Adam obeyed God, he could live forever. But if Adam took even one bite from that tree's fruit, God said he would die someday.

Adam was lonely, for he was the only person in all the world. So God decided to make another person who would live with Adam and help him. God put Adam to sleep. Then God took one of Adam's ribs and made a woman from it. When God brought the woman to Adam, she became his wife. And Adam named her Eve.

God looked at all he had made in six days, and he was very pleased.

On the seventh day, God rested. It was a quiet day, different from all the others—a holy day of rest.

- - - - - - - - - - - - - - - - - - - - - - - - - - - - - - - - - - - - - - - - - -

**Look at the picture on page 2 and name some things that God created.**

**How did God make Adam?**

**What did God tell Adam he could do?**

**What did Adam need to do so he could live forever?**

**How did God make Eve?**

- - - - - - - - - - - - - - - - - - - - - - - - - - - - - - - - - - - - - - - - - -

STORY 2

# *The World's Saddest Day*

### GENESIS 3; ROMANS 5:12-16

Satan is a wicked spirit. He tries to make people do things that are wrong. He came to Eve in the Garden of Eden. He was in the shape of a serpent.

Satan asked Eve, "Did God really tell you not to eat the fruit of any of the trees in the Garden?"

"We may eat any of it except from one tree," she replied. "We are not to eat the fruit of the tree in the middle of the Garden. God said that if we do, we will start growing old and die."

"That's not true!" Satan told her. "It won't hurt you at all! Really, it's good and will make you wise."

*Adam and Eve were afraid of God and tried to hide.*

Eve should have gone away and should not have listened to Satan. But instead, she went over and looked at the tree. The fruit looked good! So she ate some fruit. She gave some to Adam, and he ate it too. Then they were afraid of God and tried to hide.

God was angry. He told the serpent, "You will have to crawl in the dust all your life."

God told the woman, "You will have pain when your children are born."

God told Adam, "You will have to work hard to get food to eat. And someday you will die. Your body will become dust again."

But God still loved Adam and Eve. So he made clothes for them before he sent them out of the beautiful garden. He also promised to send a Savior. That Savior was God's Son, Jesus, who came years later to die for everyone's sins. (Perhaps you already know that after Jesus died, he came back to life. Now he lives in heaven with God the Father.)

All of us do bad things. We sin, just like Adam and Eve did. But God forgives us if we ask him to, because Jesus died to take away our sins.

Did Adam and Eve obey God or Satan?

How did God punish Adam and Eve?

When God was angry, how did he still show his love?

When we do bad things, what can we ask God to do?

STORY 3

# *The First Family Fight*

GENESIS 4:1-16

After God sent Adam and Eve out of the Garden, he gave them two sons. Cain became a farmer, planting crops. Abel was a shepherd with a flock of sheep.

The two brothers both sinned—they did things that were wrong. But Abel pleased God. So we know he was sorry about his sins. One day Abel offered his best lamb as a gift to God. He put the lamb on an altar made of stones. This gift was called a sacrifice. By giving God his best lamb, Abel showed God that he loved him.

God was pleased that Abel worshiped him like this.

One day God would send his Son, Jesus, into the world. Jesus would become a very special kind of sacrifice. He would die to save us from having to take the blame for our sins. Then he would come back to life.

Abel's brother, Cain, did not please God. He did not turn from his sins. The offering he brought

*Cain took his anger out on Abel.*

was from his garden, but he did not bring the best things from his garden.

When Cain learned that God had accepted Abel's sacrifice but not his, he was angry with God. But God said that if Cain would worship him in the right way, he would accept Cain's gift.

Cain, who was still angry with God, took his anger out on Abel. One day in a field, Cain killed Abel.

God called to Cain, "Where is Abel, your brother?"

"How should I know?" Cain answered. "Am I supposed to look after my brother?"

But God had seen what Cain had done. So God said Cain would always have to wander from place to place. He would have to keep looking for places where crops would grow. Cain was afraid that people would try to hurt him. But God still loved Cain and said he would never let that happen.

What gift did Abel give God?

What did Cain offer to God?

Before he would accept Cain's gift, what did God want Cain to do?

What terrible thing is Cain getting ready to do in the picture on page 7?

Afterward, what did God say would happen to Cain? What would not happen?

STORY 4

# A Long, Long Time to Live

## GENESIS 5

Cain and Abel's father and mother, Adam and Eve, lived for many years after the fight between their first two sons. When Adam was 930 years old, he died. His body became dust again. That's what God had said would happen because Adam and Eve sinned in the Garden of Eden.

Before Adam and Eve died, they had many children. The children grew up and had children too. Then those children grew up and had children, until there were many, many people in the world.

*Methuselah lived longer than anyone else has lived.*

One of those people was Enoch. He walked with God. That means he loved God and thought about God all the time. It was as if he and God walked together like friends. Enoch listened to what God said and always tried to please and obey him. When Enoch was 365 years old, God did a wonderful thing for him. God took Enoch right up to heaven! So he didn't die like other men. God just took Enoch away to live with him.

Enoch had a son named Methuselah, who lived to be 969 years old. Methuselah is known as the oldest man who ever lived.

What special thing happened to Enoch?

Who was the oldest man who ever lived?

How old was he when he died?

STORY 5

# Noah Is Safe in a Boat

### GENESIS 6:1–9:17

As the years went by, the world became very wicked. People didn't even try to obey God. So God said he would send a flood to drown all living things.

But one good man named Noah loved God and always wanted to please him. God loved Noah too, and told him about the flood so he could get ready for it.

God told Noah, "I want you to build a huge boat." God said to make it as high as a three-story house, with many large rooms. It was to have a long window all around it and a big door on the side.

It took Noah more than one hundred years to build the boat. But as you know, at that time people lived much longer than they do now.

When the boat was finished, God told Noah to bring his wife, his three sons, and each son's wife into the boat. God also said to bring fathers and

*God took care of Noah, his family, and all the animals.*

mothers for each kind of bird, animal, and insect. God said that in one week he would send a rain that would last forty days and forty nights. A flood would come, and everyone outside the boat would be drowned.

When all were safely inside, God closed the door.

Seven days later it began to rain. The rain poured down for forty days and forty nights, just as God had said it would. The creeks, the rivers, and the great oceans all began to rise, and water covered the land. Higher and higher the water rose, with the boat floating on it.

What about the people who wouldn't obey God? Now it was too late for them to get into the boat.

But God took care of Noah and all those who were with him. Finally the rain stopped, and the water began to go down again.

After Noah had been in the boat for 150 days—almost half a year—the boat rested on top of Mount Ararat. Two and a half months later, the flood had gone down even more.

Finally the ground was dry. So God told Noah and his family to come out of the boat. He said to let out all the animals and insects and birds, too.

Then Noah built an altar. He gave animals and birds to the Lord God to thank God for saving him and his family from the Flood.

God promised that he would never send another flood to drown all living things. As proof, he gave Noah a sign—a beautiful rainbow in the sky. Whenever he saw it, Noah would remember God's promise not to send a flood like that again. When we see a rainbow, we can remember God's promise too.

................................................................................

**Why did God send the Flood?**

**What people did Noah bring onto the boat?**

**What else did Noah bring onto the boat?**

**How long did it rain?**

**What can you think about when you see a rainbow?**

................................................................................

# A Tall Tower

## GENESIS 10–11

After the Flood ended, God gave children to Noah's sons and their wives. Noah's grandchildren grew up and had children too, until the world was full of people again.

These people acted just like the people before the Flood. They kept on doing all sorts of bad things. Their hearts were not filled with love for God.

There was only one language at that time. Everyone in all the world could understand everyone else. One day the people said to each other, "Let's build a tower as high as heaven!" The people were proud and wanted to show how great they were. But it is sinful to be proud.

The Lord came down from heaven and decided to stop the people from building the tower. So he made them start speaking different languages! One man would ask another for a hammer, but the other man couldn't understand him. This made them angry with each other, and soon they stopped working and went home.

When people couldn't understand each other anymore, they got all mixed up. The word *Babel* means "mixed up." So the tower was called the tower of Babel, and it was never finished.

Different groups of people moved away from other groups who didn't speak their language. That is why different languages are spoken in different parts of the world today. We now have thousands of languages, like English, Spanish, French, German, Afrikaans, Russian, Arabic, and Korean.

Why did the people want to build a tower?

What did God do to stop the people?

Why was the tower called the tower of Babel?

What language do you speak? Can you name some others?

*"Let's build a tower as high as heaven!"*

*Abram told Sarai, "God will show us where he wants us to live."*

# A New Home for Abram

### GENESIS 11:27–12:10

Far away in the land of Ur (which was in the country we call Iraq), there lived a seventy-five-year-old man named Abram. The people of Ur worshiped idols of wood and stone. This was very wrong, for God had said people must worship only him. God told Abram, "Leave this country. I will show you another land where I want you to live."

So Abram left home with his wife, Sarai, his nephew Lot, and his servants. Even though he didn't know how far he would have to go or how long he would have to travel, he believed God would take care of him.

Abram and the others had to cross wide rivers and a dry, lonely desert. Yet God took care of them and brought them safely to the Promised Land of Canaan. Today we call it the land of Israel.

"I will give this whole country to you," God told Abram. "It will belong to you and to your children forever." Then Abram built an altar and worshiped God.

God kept Abram safe from other people living in the new land who might have hurt him. But when crops didn't grow well in the fields, the people had little to eat. So Abram and his family went away for a while to a country called Egypt, waiting until there was more food in Canaan.

Why did God want Abram to move away from the people of Ur?

What was the name of the new land where God safely brought Abram?

What is the country called today?

# *Abram Shares His Land*

## GENESIS 13; 17

After some time Abram and Lot and their families returned to Canaan from Egypt. Abram went to the place where he had built an altar and worshiped God again.

Abram now owned many cows, goats, and sheep. Lot had many animals too. The men who took care of Lot's animals began to fight with the men who took care of Abram's animals. Abram talked to Lot about it. Abram could have said, "This is my land, Lot. God has given it to me, so you must move away." But Abram didn't do that. He was kind to Lot and said, "Let's not have any fighting between us."

Then Abram divided the land with Lot. Abram gave Lot first choice, even though he didn't need to—it was Abram's land, for God had given it to him.

Lot chose the best part of the land—the valley by the Jordan River. After Lot had moved to his new home, the Lord said to Abram, "I will give you all of the good land Lot chose. Lot lives there now, but someday it will all be yours!"

God also told Abram he was going to change Abram's name to Abraham and Sarai's name to Sarah. He would give them so many children and grandchildren and great-grandchildren that they would become a great nation. God's promise came true. Today we call Abraham's family the Jewish people.

---

Why couldn't Abram and Lot live in the same place?

What did Abram do for Lot that was kind?

What special promise did God make to Abram?

What new names did God give to Abram and Sarai?

---

*Abram gave Lot first choice.*

# God Visits and Isaac Is Born

### GENESIS 17:1–18:15; 21:1-7

One hot day Abraham was sitting at the entrance of his tent. He looked up and saw three men walking toward him, so he ran to meet them. He bowed low, for that was the way to welcome strangers in that land.

Abraham invited the men to rest in the shade of a tree while he brought some water for their tired feet. In those days people either went barefoot or wore sandals, so their feet became hot and dusty. When guests came, it was important to give them water to wash their feet.

Abraham ran to the tent and told his wife, Sarah, "Quick, bake some bread." Next he ran out to where the cows were and selected a fat calf for roast beef.

When the meat was ready, Abraham set it before the three men. He also brought them yogurt and bread and milk. The visitors had a picnic beneath the tree while Abraham stood nearby to serve them.

"Where is Sarah?" they asked.

"My wife is in the tent," Abraham answered.

One of the visitors said, "Next year I'll come back around this time, and Sarah will have a son."

Sarah was inside the tent, but she heard those words. And she began

*God gave Abraham and Sarah a son, just as he had promised them.*

to laugh. After all, she was an old woman—around ninety years old. She was much too old to have a baby!

Now I must tell you that the three men were really not men at all. Two of them were angels, and the other one was God. Could God look and talk like a man? Yes, several times in the Bible he appeared in the form of a man and talked with someone.

When God heard Sarah laugh, he said to Abraham, "Is anything too hard for the Lord? Just as I said, I will return about a year from now. Then Sarah will have a son."

The next year God gave Abraham and Sarah a baby son, just as he had promised them. Abraham named him Isaac, for that is the name God told Abraham to give his baby boy.

Abraham was one hundred years old and Sarah was over ninety years old when Isaac was born! As Isaac grew to be a young boy, God told Abraham that Isaac would grow up and have children. It would be through him that their family would grow into a great nation.

................................................................

**Who came and talked to Abraham?**

**What promise did one of the visitors make?**

**When did the promise come true?**

**Who is in the picture?**

................................................................

STORY 10

# *A Wife for Isaac*

### GENESIS 23–24

Sarah died when she was 127 years old. Her husband, Abraham, missed her. Their son, Isaac, missed her too. But now Isaac had become a full-grown man and wanted to get married.

Abraham didn't want his son to marry any of the girls who lived nearby. These girls worshiped idols instead of God. Abraham wanted Isaac to marry a girl from the faraway country where their relatives lived. So Abraham asked his oldest servant to go to that country and bring back a girl for Isaac to marry.

The servant loaded ten of Abraham's camels with beautiful presents and began the long trip. After many days he finally came to the place where Abraham's relatives lived. He made the camels kneel down by a well outside the city.

It was evening, and the young women were all coming out to draw water from the well. The servant told God that he would ask one of the young women for some water from her pitcher. If she answered him with a smile and said she would water his camels too, he would know she was the one God had chosen to be Isaac's wife.

While he was still praying, a beautiful girl named Rebekah came to the well. The servant ran over to her and said, "Please give me a drink from your pitcher."

"Certainly, sir," she replied. "And I'll water your camels, too!" So she did.

Then the old man gave Rebekah a large gold ring and two gold bracelets. He asked if there was room at her father's house for him and his servants to spend the night. Rebekah told him who her father and her grandparents were. She also said there was plenty of room.

When the servant heard who her family was, he knew for sure that she was the right one for Isaac. He thanked God for helping him to find the right girl.

Rebekah's brother, Laban, helped the old man unload the camels and feed them.

As the servant ate supper with Rebekah's family, he asked them if they would let Rebekah go with him to marry Isaac. They said yes, since it was the Lord who had brought him.

When Abraham's servant heard this, he worshiped the Lord again. He brought out more beautiful jewelry and beautiful clothes for Rebekah. He gave her mother and her brother presents too.

*Abraham's servant met a kind young woman named Rebekah.*

The next morning Rebekah was ready to leave. She got on a camel and followed Abraham's servant all the way to Isaac's tent. Isaac loved Rebekah very much, and she became his wife.

How did Abraham's servant know that Rebekah was the right girl for Isaac?

What gifts did the servant have for her?

Where did Abraham's servant take Rebekah?

Do you think it was hard for Rebekah to move so far away?

STORY 11

# Esau's Mistake

## GENESIS 25:19-34

After Isaac and Rebekah were married, God gave them twin sons! The babies' names were Esau and Jacob. Esau was born first, and Jacob was born a few minutes later. So Esau was the older one.

In those days the oldest son in every family had what was called the birthright. This meant that when his father died, he would get more money and other things than his brothers and sisters. In fact, he would get two times as much as the other children.

In Isaac's family Esau was born first, so he had the birthright.

When Esau and Jacob grew up, Esau became a hunter. He went out into the fields and woods to kill deer. He always brought the meat home to his father, Isaac. How his father loved that meat!

Jacob stayed at home, probably helping to care for his father's sheep and goats.

One day Jacob was cooking some good food when Esau came in from his hunting. Esau was tired and hungry, so he asked Jacob for some food. Jacob said he would give him the food if Esau gave him his birthright!

Esau didn't care about his birthright at the time, so he told Jacob he could have it. Then Jacob gave him some food.

It was wrong for Esau to give away the birthright God had given him. It was wrong, too, for Jacob to take it.

What was Esau going to get from his birthright someday?

What wrong thing did Esau do?

What wrong thing did Jacob do?

*Esau gave up his birthright for some food.*

# Is It Jacob or Esau?

GENESIS 27:1-28:5

Isaac was getting old and couldn't see anymore. He told his oldest son, Esau, to go out into the field and hunt for a deer.

"Cook the meat the way I like it," said Isaac. "Then I will bless you." He meant that he would ask God to be kind to Esau and give him many good things.

Rebekah didn't want her husband, Isaac, to give the special blessing to Esau, even though he was their oldest son. She wanted Jacob to have the blessing.

When Esau had gone to hunt for deer, Rebekah told Jacob to kill two goats. She cooked the meat so it tasted like deer meat. Then she gave some of Esau's clothes to Jacob. And she put goatskins on the back of his arms and neck so Jacob would feel hairy like his brother. She told him to take the food to his father and to say that he was Esau.

Because Isaac couldn't see, he asked if it really was Esau. Jacob said, "Yes, I'm Esau. And I have brought the deer meat."

His father put his hands on Jacob and felt the hairy goatskins. Then Isaac smelled the clothes Jacob was wearing. And he believed it must be Esau. Of course, it was Jacob, and not Esau at all. Isaac ate the food and blessed Jacob. Isaac prayed for Jacob, but he thought he was praying for Esau. He prayed that God would help his son grow good crops in his fields. And he prayed for this son to be in charge of the family.

Right after Jacob left the tent, Esau came in with a deer. He cooked the meat and took it to his father.

Isaac asked, "Who are you?"

Esau answered, "I am Esau, and I have the meat you told me to get for you."

Isaac began to tremble. "But I just gave your blessing to someone else. Who was it?" he asked. Isaac knew the answer to his own question. Jacob had stolen Esau's blessing.

Esau cried and begged his father to bless him, too. Isaac did, but he had already promised the best things to Jacob.

Esau hated Jacob and planned to kill him someday.

Rebekah knew Esau was angry. She told Jacob to go away to the country where she used to live, to the home of her brother, Laban. Esau would not be able to hurt Jacob there.

Rebekah reminded her husband, Isaac, that the girls who lived nearby didn't love God. She got Isaac to agree that Jacob must not marry a Canaanite girl. He blessed Jacob again. He told Jacob to marry one of his mother's relatives in their country.

*Isaac prayed for Jacob, but he thought he was praying for Esau.*

Then Isaac sent Jacob away to that far-off land. It was the same land where Abraham's servant had found Rebekah, Jacob and Esau's mother.

....................................................................................................

**Who did Jacob pretend he was?**

**Who got the first blessing from Isaac?**

**What did Esau plan to do to Jacob?**

**Where did Isaac and Rebekah send Jacob?**

....................................................................................................

*During the night Jacob had a dream.*

# A Stairway to Heaven

### GENESIS 28:5, 10-22

Jacob began traveling to the country where his mother's relatives lived. He knew that his Uncle Laban lived there.

When the sun went down, Jacob found a good place to sleep outdoors. Using a stone for a pillow, he went to sleep.

During the night he had a dream. He thought he saw some stairs reaching all the way up to heaven. Angels were going up and down the steps. God stood at the top of the stairs. He said he was going to give this land to Jacob and his children. God said he would be with Jacob and take care of him wherever he went. And someday God would bring Jacob safely home again.

When Jacob woke up, he knew that the dream he'd had was a special dream. God was really there and had made a wonderful promise. Jacob said, "God is here, and I didn't even know it!"

Very early the next morning, Jacob got up and worshiped the Lord. He called the place Bethel, which means "house of God."

Where did Jacob sleep on the first night of his trip?

What was Jacob's dream?

What made Jacob's dream so special?

What did Jacob do the next morning?

# Jacob Works Hard and Gets Married

GENESIS 29:1–31:16

Jacob traveled a long time until he came to a well in a field. Three flocks of sheep were lying around it, and their shepherds were with them. When all the flocks arrived, the shepherds would roll away the rock that covered the well and get water for the sheep.

Jacob asked the shepherds where they lived, and they told him they lived at Haran.

"Do you know Laban?" he asked them.

"Yes," they replied. "And look, here comes his daughter Rachel with his sheep."

Jacob went over to the well. He rolled away the stone and drew out water for Rachel's sheep. Then he kissed her. When he explained that he was her aunt Rebekah's son, she ran and told her father.

Laban ran out to meet his nephew. He gave Jacob a warm welcome and brought him home. After about a month, Laban asked Jacob to stay and work for him.

By this time Jacob was in love with Rachel. He told Laban he would work for him for seven years if he could marry Rachel afterward.

*Jacob worked for seven years so he could marry Rachel.*

Laban was delighted. So Jacob worked for him for the next seven years. But when the time was up, Laban tricked Jacob into marrying Rachel's older sister, Leah. Laban took Leah to Jacob's tent at night when it was so dark that Jacob couldn't see who it was. Laban did that because he thought the oldest daughter should be married first.

A week later Jacob was allowed to marry Rachel, but he had to promise to work for her father seven more years. This was unfair, but Jacob agreed to do it because of his love for Rachel.

After many years, Jacob had a large family. He wanted to take his family back home to the land of Canaan. But Laban wouldn't let Jacob go.

One day Laban's sons said that Jacob had stolen their father's sheep and that was why he was so rich. After that, Laban was not as friendly as he used to be.

Then God told Jacob to return home to the land of Canaan. God said he would be with Jacob and keep him safe.

Jacob told Rachel and Leah to meet him in the field where he was caring for his flock. He told them that their father wasn't friendly to him anymore and that the Lord had told him to go back to Canaan.

Rachel and Leah agreed he must do whatever the Lord wanted him to do.

- - - - - - - - - - - - - - - - - - - - - - - - - - - - - - - - - - - - - - - - - -

**What was the name of the girl Jacob met at the well?**

**Who was Leah?**

**What did Laban make Jacob do that was unfair?**

**What did God promise to do for Jacob and his big family on their trip back to Jacob's home?**

- - - - - - - - - - - - - - - - - - - - - - - - - - - - - - - - - - - - - - - - - -

*Jacob and Esau were glad to be friends again.*

# Jacob's Secret Escape

### GENESIS 31:17 – 33:17

Jacob put his family on camels and started back toward the land of Canaan.

Laban was away from home when Jacob left. When someone told Laban about it three days later, he was angry. But that night, in a dream, God told Laban not to hurt Jacob or even speak to him in anger.

It took seven days for Laban to catch up with Jacob in the hills. Laban said, "Let's be friends and promise that we will never hurt each other."

Jacob agreed, and they made a huge pile of stones to remind them of their promise.

Jacob then built an altar and offered a sacrifice to God. That night he and Laban and the men who were with them ate together and camped together.

Early the next morning Laban kissed Rachel and Leah and their children good-bye and blessed them. Then he went back home.

As Jacob and his family traveled on toward Canaan, some angels met them. Jacob knew then that God was still with him, just as he had promised he would always be.

Jacob sent messengers to tell Esau what had happened while he was away. Jacob was still afraid of Esau, even though it had been twenty years since he had stolen Esau's blessing.

Jacob's messengers returned with the scary news that Esau was coming to meet him with four hundred men. Then Jacob was really afraid. He divided his sheep, goats, camels, and men into two groups. If Esau attacked one group, the other group might escape.

Jacob prayed and asked God to keep him and his family safe from Esau. He thanked the Lord for being so kind to him. When he had left Canaan twenty years earlier, he had been poor, but God had made him rich. He thanked God for this.

The next morning Jacob sent some of his animals as a present to Esau. He sent 220 goats, 220 sheep, 30 camels with their colts, 40 cows, 10 bulls, and 30 donkeys.

Esau ran to meet his twin brother and put his arms around him. They both cried. But they were glad to be friends again.

----

After Jacob and his family left Laban, what did God say to Laban in a dream?

How many years had it been since Jacob stole Esau's blessing?

How did Jacob and Esau show each other they wanted to be friends again?

----

STORY 16

# Joseph's Coat

### GENESIS 35; 37:1-4

Jacob brought his family back to his home in Canaan. On the way, Rachel had a baby, a son Jacob named Benjamin. But Rachel died soon afterward. Jacob was terribly sad, because he loved Rachel very much.

Little Benjamin had a big brother named Joseph. Their father was Jacob and their mother was Rachel. Joseph and Benjamin were the youngest boys in a family with twelve sons!

When Joseph was seventeen years old, he went out into the fields one day. He went to help his ten older brothers, who were taking care of the sheep and the goats. But while he was there, he saw his brothers do something that was wrong. That night when he got home, he told his father. This was a good thing to do, for his father could talk to his brothers about what they had done. Then maybe they would not do it again. But of course his brothers were angry with him for telling on them.

Jacob was an old man when Joseph was born. So Jacob loved Joseph more than he loved Joseph's big brothers. Joseph was Jacob's favorite son.

*Joseph wore the beautiful coat Jacob had made for him.*

One day Jacob had a beautiful coat made for Joseph. It was a finer piece of clothing than any of Joseph's older brothers had. So Joseph's brothers became very jealous. They hated Joseph and never said one kind word to him after that.

.................................................................................

**What did Joseph do when he was seventeen years old?**

**What did Jacob give Joseph to wear?**

**How did Joseph's older brothers act when their father gave Joseph a beautiful coat?**

.................................................................................

STORY 17

# Joseph's Dreams

### GENESIS 37:5-36

One night after Joseph's father gave him the beautiful coat, Joseph had a strange dream. The next morning he told his family about it.

"In my dream," he said, "all of us were out in the field tying bundles of grain stalks. Then your bundles stood around mine and bowed to it!"

This dream made his brothers angry. Did Joseph think they should bow to him as though he were their king?

Then Joseph dreamed that the sun, the moon, and eleven stars bowed to him. His brothers were angrier than ever. They knew they were the eleven stars. The sun and moon must have meant their father and mother would bow to Joseph too.

Soon after this the brothers took their father's sheep to find grass for the sheep to eat. They walked for several days to get there.

Later Jacob said to Joseph, "Go and see how your brothers are getting along." So Joseph went to find them.

*One night Joseph had a strange dream.*

When his brothers saw him coming, they began talking to each other about killing him. They said, "Let's throw him into a well. We'll say a wild animal ate him. Then we'll see what happens to his dreams!"

Joseph's brother Reuben talked his other brothers into putting Joseph in a deep hole without hurting him. Reuben planned to come back and take Joseph out of the hole.

When Joseph got there, his brothers took away his beautiful coat and put him into the deep hole.

As they sat down to eat their lunches, they saw some men coming along on camels. These men were merchants who were taking things to sell in the country of Egypt. Joseph's brother Judah said, "Let's sell Joseph to those men!"

The other brothers agreed—all except Reuben, who wasn't there at the time. So they pulled Joseph out of the well and sold him for twenty pieces of silver. The merchants put him on a camel and took him far away to the land of Egypt.

When Reuben came back to the well to save Joseph, he exclaimed, "Joseph is gone! What shall I do now?"

The brothers killed a goat and dipped Joseph's coat in the blood. They took the coat to their father and told him they had found it on the ground.

Jacob knew it was Joseph's coat. He cried and said, "A wild animal must have eaten Joseph. He is dead." After that, Jacob told everyone he would be sad the rest of his life.

........................................................................................

What did Joseph dream about?

What did Joseph's brothers do to him?

How did the brothers make their father think a wild animal killed Joseph?

........................................................................................

# Joseph Becomes an Important Man

### GENESIS 39–41

The men who took Joseph to Egypt sold him to a man named Potiphar. Joseph became Potiphar's servant and lived in his house.

Potiphar's wife wanted Joseph to do something that was wrong, but he said no. She became angry and told her husband that Joseph had tried to hurt her. So her husband sent Joseph to jail. In the jail, God helped Joseph tell two men what their dreams meant.

Pharaoh, the king of Egypt, had some dreams too. He dreamed about seven skinny cows and seven fat cows. Then he dreamed about seven plump pieces of grain and seven dried-up pieces. He sent for Joseph and said, "I had a dream last night. No one has been able to tell me what it means, but I've heard that you can tell me."

*The farmers had to give some of their grain to Pharaoh.*

Joseph said that he could not do it, but that God would. So Pharaoh told Joseph the dream about cows and the one about grain. Joseph told the king that both dreams meant the same thing. God was telling Pharaoh there would be seven years of good crops followed by seven years when no crops would grow.

Pharaoh didn't send Joseph back to jail. Instead, he put Joseph in charge of all the land of Egypt. The king dressed Joseph in fine clothes and gave him a gold chain. Now Joseph was the governor of Egypt. He was almost as great as Pharaoh.

During the next seven years, Joseph made the farmers give some of their grain to Pharaoh. Joseph stored this grain in nearby cities.

Then the seven years of poor crops began. Soon all the people's food was gone, and they asked Pharaoh for something to eat.

Pharaoh said, "Joseph will tell you what to do."

Then Joseph opened the buildings where the grain was kept and sold it to the people.

- - - - - - - - - - - - - - - - - - - - - - - - - - - - - - - - - - - - - - - - - - - -

**Why did Potiphar put Joseph in jail?**

**Who helped Joseph to know what the king's two dreams were?**

**What was God telling Pharaoh in the dreams?**

**What did Joseph do when Pharaoh put him in charge of the land?**

- - - - - - - - - - - - - - - - - - - - - - - - - - - - - - - - - - - - - - - - - - - -

STORY 19

# Joseph's Older Brothers Come to Egypt

### GENESIS 42:1-35

Joseph's brothers were still living in the land of Canaan when crops stopped growing. Jacob, their father, said, "I hear there is grain in Egypt. Go and buy some for us."

So Joseph's ten older brothers got on their donkeys and rode for many days until they came to Egypt. They bowed down to the governor, who was in charge of selling grain. The brothers didn't recognize Joseph in his Egyptian robes, but he knew them right away.

Joseph acted as if he didn't know them. He spoke loudly and said, "You are spies. You have come to see if we are weak."

"Oh no, sir," his brothers answered. "We have come to buy food." They told him their youngest brother was with their father in the land of Canaan.

Joseph said he was sending them back to Canaan to get their youngest brother. But one of them would have to stay in Egypt. That was the only way Joseph could trust them to come back again with their youngest brother. Simeon was the brother that Joseph chose to stay behind.

The brothers said to each other that God was punishing them for selling Joseph long ago.

*Joseph's brothers traveled to Egypt to buy grain.*

Then Joseph told his servants to fill his brothers' sacks with grain. He said to put at the tops of their sacks the money they had paid for the grain.

Finally all except Simeon started traveling back home to Canaan. That night one of the men opened a sack to get some food, and there was his money! He told the other brothers. Then all of them were afraid because they didn't know how the money got there.

When the brothers came home, each one found at the top of his sack the money he had paid for the grain. Their father, Jacob, saw the money, and he was afraid too.

Why did Joseph's brothers go to Egypt?

What did the brothers do when they saw the governor?

Why didn't the brothers know that the governor was Joseph?

Which brother did Joseph keep in Egypt?

What did Joseph tell his servants to do with the brothers' money?

STORY 20

# A Big Surprise

### GENESIS 42:36–46:34

Jacob did not want to let Benjamin, his youngest son, go to Egypt. But the family needed food. So finally Jacob let all of his sons go, sending presents of honey, nuts, spices, and money for the governor.

Once again the brothers bowed down in front of Joseph, just the way Joseph had dreamed they would someday. Then Joseph said, "It's time to eat." He had the brothers sit in the order of their ages, and he gave Benjamin five times as much food as any of the others.

Joseph sent his brothers home with food. He told a servant to place Joseph's silver cup in Benjamin's sack. Then the servant chased after the brothers, found the cup, and brought them back to Joseph. He told them Benjamin would have to stay in Egypt for stealing the cup.

But Judah asked Joseph to let him stay instead. Then the other brothers could take Benjamin home to their father.

Joseph began to cry. He knew now that his brothers had learned to care for one another. He told them, "I am your brother Joseph!" How surprised they all were!

After they all hugged each other, Joseph told

*The servant found the silver cup in Benjamin's sack.*

them not to be sad about selling him to the merchants. He said it was God's plan to bring him to Egypt. Because Pharaoh had put him in charge of the grain, he could keep his family alive by giving them grain for food.

Joseph told his brothers, "Hurry home and bring my father here." So Jacob and all of his family came to live in Egypt.

Which son did Jacob finally let go to Egypt?

How did Joseph's dreams from long ago come true?

What did Judah offer to do so Benjamin could go home?

Why did Joseph say his brothers should not be sad about selling him?

*The princess felt sorry for the baby inside the*
*basket and wanted him to be her son.*

# A Princess Finds a Baby

### EXODUS 1:1-2:10

Jacob lived in Egypt until he died. Then his son Joseph and his other sons grew old and died. But their children grew up and had many children and grandchildren. After hundreds of years, there were many people in Jacob's family.

A new king began to rule over Egypt. He didn't know about Joseph, and he was afraid of Jacob's huge family. So he and his Egyptian people made slaves of Jacob's family, now known as the Israelites. The Israelites worked hard with no pay! But their families grew bigger, as God had promised.

The new king of Egypt was called the Pharaoh, just as the old king had been. He told his people that they must not let the Israelite baby boys live. But God helped the babies' families.

Now I'm going to tell you about one of those little babies. The baby's mother hid him at home while she made a basket-boat. She smeared tar on the outside of it to keep the water out. She knew the little boat would float safely on the water. And she hoped Pharaoh's soldiers would not find her baby boy.

The mother put her baby in the basket and floated it among the bushes at the edge of the river. Miriam, the baby's sister, hid nearby so she could help her brother.

Soon a princess, Pharaoh's daughter, came along and saw the little boat. When she opened the basket, she felt sorry for the baby inside and wanted him to be her son.

Miriam, the baby's sister, asked, "Should I get an Israelite woman to take care of the baby?" The princess said yes, so Miriam ran home and got her mother!

When the baby was older, the princess sent for him to come and live in her palace and be her son. She called him Moses.

Why did the baby's mother put him in a basket-boat in the water?

Who found the baby?

How did the baby's sister help him?

What did the princess name the baby?

# A Voice in a Burning Bush

### EXODUS 2:11–4:20

Moses grew up in the palace in Egypt, but he was an Israelite. One day he killed an Egyptian man who was hurting an Israelite man. Then Moses ran away to the land of Midian. He lived there for many years.

The Egyptians, who had another new Pharaoh as their king, were making the people of Israel work very hard. They were hurting the Israelites, and God felt bad for his people. So God gave Moses a job to do. This is how it happened.

One day Moses was taking care of his family's sheep. Suddenly he saw a bush on fire, but the bush didn't burn up! God called from the bush, "Moses!"

"Yes, Lord," Moses said.

God told him, "Take off your sandals, because you are standing on holy ground." Then God said he had heard the cries of the Israelites.

The Lord told Moses to go and tell the new Pharaoh, the king of Egypt, to stop hurting the

*Moses saw a bush on fire,*
*but the bush didn't burn up!*

44

Israelites. God also told Moses to lead the people out of Egypt and back to Canaan.

But Moses said no one would believe that the Lord had sent him.

God told Moses to throw his shepherd's stick on the ground. Moses did, and God changed it into a snake! Then the Lord said, "Grab it by the tail." Moses did, and it became a shepherd's stick again. God helped Moses do this miracle. He told Moses that when the Israelites saw him do it, they would believe that God had sent him.

Moses said he wasn't good at talking. God promised that Moses' brother, Aaron, could talk to Pharaoh and the people of Israel. God would tell Moses what to say, and Moses would tell Aaron what to say.

So Moses made plans to return to Egypt.

........................................................................

**What was strange about the bush Moses saw?**

**What miracle did God help Moses do?**

**Who did God say could talk to Pharaoh for Moses?**

........................................................................

STORY 23

# *Terrible Troubles*

### EXODUS 4:29-31; 7-10

Moses and his brother, Aaron, went to Egypt and talked with the Israelite leaders. God helped Moses turn his shepherd's stick into a snake. He did another miracle too. Then the leaders believed that God had sent Moses to lead them out of Egypt.

Moses and Aaron went to Pharaoh. They told him that God said, "Let my people leave Egypt." But Pharaoh said no.

So God told Moses to hit the Nile River with his shepherd's stick. The water changed to blood. Soon the Egyptians had no water to drink. But Pharaoh wouldn't let God's people go.

*The dust changed into lice, which covered the Egyptian people.*

Then God made millions of frogs come up out of the rivers and into the homes of the Egyptian people. But Pharaoh still wouldn't let the Israelite people go.

Moses told Aaron to hit the ground with his shepherd's stick, and the dust changed into small biting insects called lice. They covered the Egyptian people and the cows. But Pharaoh wouldn't let the people go.

The Lord told Moses to meet Pharaoh as he went down to the river. Again Pharaoh said no, he wouldn't let the people go. So God sent flies, and they covered the whole country. But there were no flies where the Israelites lived.

Pharaoh told Moses and Aaron, "All right, the people of Israel can go, but not far." But when Pharaoh saw that the flies were gone, he wouldn't let the people go!

Next God sent a sickness that killed the animals of the Egyptians. But the Israelites' animals stayed healthy. Pharaoh's heart grew even harder and more wicked than before, and he would not let the people go!

Then Moses and Aaron tossed ashes into the air, and sores broke out on people and animals all over Egypt.

But Pharaoh's heart was still wicked, and he wouldn't let the people go!

So God sent a hailstorm such as there had never been before. Everything out in the storm died. But no hail fell on the people of Israel!

Pharaoh sent for Moses and Aaron and said, "I have sinned. The Lord is good, but my people and I are wicked. Beg the Lord to stop the hail, and I will let you go."

When Moses prayed, the hail stopped. But Pharaoh changed his mind again and wouldn't let the people go!

Then locusts came and ate up all the crops of the Egyptians. After that, it became dark for three days where the people of Egypt lived. But in the houses of the Israelites, it was as light as usual.

Pharaoh said to Moses, "Go and worship the Lord, but don't take your sheep and cows." Moses told Pharaoh they needed their animals as gifts to God. That made Pharaoh angry. He told Moses to get away from him and never come back again.

What did God want Pharaoh to let the people of Israel do?

Can you name three or four of the terrible troubles God sent to Pharaoh and the people of Egypt?

While God was sending troubles to the Egyptians, what was happening to the Israelites?

STORY 24

# *The Worst Trouble of All*

EXODUS 11–12; 2 CORINTHIANS 5:7-8

Moses went to Pharaoh one more time. He said that God was going to send one last terrible trouble. The oldest son in every Egyptian home would die. Even Pharaoh's oldest son would die. But not one of the Israelite children would be hurt.

Moses left after he had said all of this, letting Pharaoh sit there.

Then the Lord told the Israelites to get ready to leave Egypt. He told them to ask the Egyptians for silver and gold jewelry. And the Lord would make the Egyptians want to give their jewelry to the people of Israel.

The Lord said that on the tenth day of the month each family should pick a lamb to eat. They should kill it on the fourth evening after that. Then they should sprinkle the lamb's blood on each side and on top of the doors to their homes. They were to stay in their houses and roast the lamb, God said. And everyone in the house was to eat some of it.

As they ate they had to be dressed to travel, with their shoes on and their walking sticks in their hands. They were to eat in a hurry, for that night the oldest son in every Egyptian home would die. And at last Pharaoh would really let the Israelites go.

God promised that he would pass over the houses with blood on the door. No one would die there. So the Israelites' lamb supper that night would always be called the Lord's "Passover."

Everything happened just as God said. Pharaoh got up in the night with all his people. There was a cry of great sadness through all the land, for in every Egyptian home the oldest son was dead.

Pharaoh called for Moses and Aaron and told them to leave Egypt at once and to take all the people of Israel with them. "Take your sheep and cows too," he said, "and leave tonight." The Egyptians were afraid they would all die, so they begged the Israelites to leave right away.

God's people left Egypt that night, carrying their clothes on their shoulders. The Egyptians gave them silver and gold jewelry, and fine clothes, too. So the Israelites went away with great riches.

*The lamb's blood was sprinkled on the top and sides of the Israelites' doors.*

The lamb that was killed in every Israelite home that night was in some ways like Jesus, our Savior. The lamb died for the people, and its blood saved them. That is what happened again many years later, when Jesus came as the Lamb of God. He died for each of us. Then he came back to life! And now he saves all of us who love him.

Just as God did not punish those who had lamb's blood around their doors, so it will be when Jesus comes again. He will not punish those whose hearts have been made clean from sin. Those who love Jesus are clean because of the blood he gave when he died.

What made the Egyptian families feel sad and afraid?

What did God tell the Israelites to do so that he would pass over their homes and keep them safe?

How is Jesus like the lambs that died that night?

STORY 25

# A Pillar of Cloud and Fire

### EXODUS 13:17–15:21

At last the people of Israel were free, and God led them toward the Red Sea. As they traveled, God went ahead of them in a cloud to show them the way. The cloud was shaped like a pillar reaching up toward heaven. At night the cloud became a pillar of fire. It gave the people light so they could travel whenever God wanted them to, day or night.

Almost as soon as the Israelites left Egypt, Pharaoh and his officers were sorry they had let them go. "Why did we ever let them get away from us?" they said.

So Pharaoh and his army got into their chariots and chased after the people of Israel. They caught up with them as the Israelites were camping by the Red Sea. The Israelites saw the Egyptians coming and were afraid. They blamed Moses for getting them into this trouble. But Moses told them not to be afraid. "Wait and see what the Lord will do for you," he said. "God will fight for you, so you won't need to do a thing."

When Pharaoh and his army were very close, the pillar of cloud in front of God's people moved behind them. It came between them and Pharaoh's army. During the night the pillar was dark on the side where Pharaoh was. But the side that faced Israel was as bright as fire!

The Lord said to Moses, "Tell my people to start marching to the sea. When they get there, point your shepherd's stick toward the sea, and a path through the water will open up in front of you. Then my people will go across on dry ground!"

*God went ahead of the Israelites in a cloud to show them the way.*

51

So Moses did what God had told him to. And the water opened up ahead of them. It was piled high like walls on each side of the people, so they could safely walk across the bottom of the sea on dry ground!

The next morning Pharaoh and his army started across between the walls of water. But the Lord made the wheels come off the Egyptian chariots, so they came to a quick stop.

"Turn around! Let's get out of here!" the Egyptians shouted. "The Lord is fighting against us. He is for the Israelites."

But before the Egyptians could get out, the Lord told Moses to point his rod toward the sea again. When he did, the water came back together. It covered all of the Egyptians.

Moses and the Israelites were safe on the other side of the Red Sea. Moses' sister, Miriam, played a tambourine. And God's people joyfully sang a song of praise to the Lord for saving them from Pharaoh.

How did God show his people the way to go?

How did God help his people get across the Red Sea?

What did Miriam and all of God's people do when they were safe?

# *Food from Heaven*

### EXODUS 16

The Israelites were walking across a big desert to the Promised Land. They got upset with Moses because they were hungry. They said that when they were in Egypt they had plenty of food.

God told Moses he would send meat for the people that evening and as much bread as they wanted in the morning. Then they would know that God was taking care of them.

That evening huge flocks of birds called quail flew into camp. The people ate them for supper.

The next morning small white flakes were all over the ground. They tasted like bread with honey. The people called this food "manna," which means, "What is it?"

"This is the bread God promised you," Moses said.

God told the people to gather what they needed for each day. He said there would be more food every morning. The Lord wanted them to trust him one day at a time for their food. Some of the people didn't obey. They gathered enough for two days. But the extra manna spoiled, and worms crawled around in it.

On the sixth day God sent two times as much manna as on other days. That was because the next day was the Sabbath day, when God told everyone to rest. On that day there was no manna. So on the sixth day the people could save manna for the next day and it didn't spoil.

The Israelites ate manna every day for forty years!

...................................................................

**What did God give the people to eat for supper?**

**What did God send them in the morning six days a week?**

**How long did the people eat this food?**

...................................................................

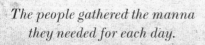

*The people gathered the manna they needed for each day.*

# The Ten Commandments

EXODUS 19–20; 24; DEUTERONOMY 5;
MATTHEW 5:21-22

The Israelites came to the bottom of Mount Sinai two months after leaving Egypt. Moses went to the top of the mountain, where God gave him Ten Commandments. These commandments are for everyone to follow.

1. You must not have any other god but me.
   *This means that we must love God more than anyone or anything else.*

2. You must not make any idol, or bow down to one, or worship it.
   *Some people make statues, or idols, from wood or stone. They believe that the idols are gods. But God is the one who created us, and we are to worship no one but him.*

3. You must not use the name of the Lord your God in the wrong way.
   *Whenever we speak God's name, we must do it with respect, remembering how great and holy a name it is. We are not to swear.*

4. Remember to keep the Sabbath day holy.
   *God tells his people not to work on the seventh day. This is because God rested on the seventh day after his six days of creation.*

5. Honor your father and your mother.
   *Next to God, the most important people to obey are parents. We honor them by doing what they tell us.*

6. You must not commit murder.
   *We must not kill other people. When God's Son, Jesus, came to earth many years later, he said that hating someone is as bad as killing that person.*

God gave Moses two tablets of stone with the Ten Commandments written on them.

7. You must not commit adultery.

    *When a married man sleeps with a woman who is not his wife, or a married woman sleeps with a man who is not her husband, it is called adultery.*

8. You must not steal.

    *We must not take anything that belongs to someone else. If you have ever done this, God says you should give it back or pay for it.*

9. You must not tell lies.

    *This means we must never say anything about another person that isn't true. And don't leave out a little or add a little to make it different from the real truth.*

10. You must not covet or long to have what belongs to your neighbor.

    *We must not be upset when we can't have things God gives to other people.*

Everyone heard loud thunder and a trumpet blast. The people saw lightning and smoke. And they were afraid. Moses came down from the mountain and told them God hadn't come to hurt them—he just came to show his power.

Moses once again gave the people the instructions God had given him. All of the people said together, "We will obey God. We will do everything he commands us to do."

........................................................................................................

**Can you name three or four of the Ten Commandments? Read the rest of them.**

**When Moses told the people God's commands, what did the people say they would do?**

**What did God write the Ten Commandments on? (See the picture on page 55 and the words below it.)**

........................................................................................................

# A Special House for God

## EXODUS 25–28

While Moses was on Mount Sinai, God told him that the people should build a Tabernacle. This would be a beautiful tent that was like a church, where they could worship God. The Tabernacle would be easy to take apart and put together again so the people could carry it with them on their trip to the land of Canaan.

God also told Moses to make a special box to be placed inside the Tabernacle. This beautiful box, called the Ark of the Covenant, would be covered with gold. Moses was to put inside the Ark the two stone tablets with the Ten Commandments written on them. On the cover of the Ark there would be two gold angels.

The frame of the Tabernacle would be made of boards covered with gold.

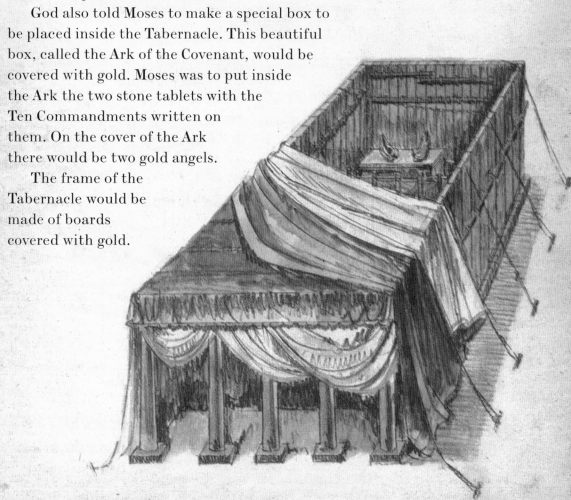

*The Tabernacle was a beautiful tent where the people could worship God.*

The frame would be covered with cloth that was blue, purple, and red. And a beautiful curtain would divide the Tabernacle into two rooms.

There would be a little yard with a wall of curtains all around the Tabernacle. An altar would stand in the yard.

The Lord said that Aaron and his sons would be priests. They would offer to God the animals that the people brought. Aaron, the high priest, would be in charge.

God said Aaron was to wear a long robe. Over the robe he would have a blue coat. Hanging from the coat would be blue, purple, and red yarn made to look like fruit. Aaron was also to wear a vest with twelve beautiful jewels on it. On his head Aaron would wear a turban with a band of gold. These words were to be written on the band: "Set apart as holy to the Lord."

---

Why did God want the Tabernacle to be easy to take apart and put together again?

How was the Tabernacle like your church building? How was it different?

What was special about Aaron? Tell about his clothes.

---

STORY 29

# A Gold Calf

### EXODUS 31:18–34:35

When the Lord had finished talking with Moses, he gave him the two tablets of stone on which he had written the Ten Commandments. Moses had been with God on Mount Sinai for forty days and forty nights, learning about all the things God wanted his people to do.

Meanwhile, the people of Israel were camped at the foot of the mountain. They were tired of waiting for Moses. So they said to Aaron,

*The people bowed to the gold calf and said it was their god.*

"We don't know what has become of Moses. We want to worship idols, like all the other nations do."

"All right," Aaron said. "Bring me the gold earrings that belong to your wives and children." Aaron melted the earrings in a fire and poured the gold into a big lump, which he made into the shape of a calf.

The people bowed to the gold calf and said it was their god. Aaron built an altar in front of it. Early the next morning, the people gave offerings to the calf instead of to the Lord. They had a big party, eating and getting drunk and dancing around the calf.

God told Moses, who was still on the mountain, "Quick! Go back down. The people have done a very wicked thing. They have made a calf and are worshiping it. They are calling it their god."

Moses hurried down the mountain with the two tablets of stone in his hands. His helper, Joshua, was with him. As they came near the camp, Moses saw the people dancing in front of the gold calf. In great anger he threw the two tablets of stone down the mountain, and they broke into many pieces.

Moses ran the rest of the way down the mountain. He smashed the calf and ground the gold into powder. Then he threw the powder into the water and made the people drink it.

A terrible punishment from the Lord came upon his people because of their sin. About three thousand of them died that day.

The next day Moses said that he would pray for the people. So he told God that the people had sinned terribly because they had made a gold idol and worshiped it. But he asked God to forgive his people and begged God to stay with them. The Lord listened to Moses' prayer and finally promised to forgive his people and stay with them.

Then God told Moses to make two stone tablets like the ones he had broken. God said he would write the Ten Commandments again.

So Moses made two new tablets of rock, just like those he had broken. He went back to the top of Mount Sinai early in the morning, carrying the tablets. And the Lord came down in a cloud. Moses prayed again that the Lord would forgive the people of Israel.

God promised that he would do wonderful things for the Israelites. He would drive out the wicked people of Canaan to make room for his people to live there instead.

················································································

What did the people of Israel ask Aaron to make for them?

What two things did Moses do to show how upset he was with the people?

When Moses asked God to forgive the people and stay with them, what did God say he would do?

················································································

STORY 30

# *Workers Build the Tabernacle*

### EXODUS 35–40; LEVITICUS 16; HEBREWS 7

Now it was time to build the Tabernacle. Moses invited the people to bring their gifts of gold, silver, bronze, wood, and whatever else was needed. Each family gladly brought gifts. Finally there was enough, but the people kept bringing more. Moses had to tell them to stop!

Workers chosen by God made curtains for the roof and walls of the Tabernacle. They also made a curtain to hang inside it, and another for the entrance. They covered board frames with gold. They put cloth over the whole Tabernacle.

Then the workers made Aaron's beautiful clothes. Gold bells at the bottom of his robe chimed as Aaron went in and out of the Tabernacle.

One worker made the Ark of the Covenant. This beautiful box with two gold angels on top was the most important part of the Tabernacle because it was a special place to meet with God.

When the Tabernacle was finished, the cloud pillar that had led the people came down and covered it. God's glory filled the Tabernacle.

*Each family gladly brought gifts to help build the Tabernacle.*

The Ark was in the inner room. This room was called the Most Holy Place. The Lord told Moses that only Aaron, the high priest, could go in there. And Aaron could go there only once every year.

Aaron offered gifts or sacrifices for his sins and for the sins of the people. Many years later, Jesus, the Savior, was born. After he grew up, he did not offer sacrifices. But he became a sacrifice when he died on a cross for our sins. Aaron is not alive today and cannot pray for us. But Jesus came back to life. Then he went up to heaven. Jesus is alive in heaven, and every day he is asking God to forgive us when we pray.

How did families help with the building of the Tabernacle?

What did Aaron offer God for the sins of the people?

How did Jesus become a gift or sacrifice to God?

STORY 31

# *Three Holidays*

### LEVITICUS 23

The Lord told the people of Israel to have several religious holidays each year. Here are three of them.

The first was the Passover. This celebration was to remind God's people of the night their families came out of Egypt. Each year God wanted them to remember how he had passed over the Israelite homes in Egypt and had kept their families safe. For the Passover holiday, the people were to eat lamb during the night, just as they did that first time. For seven days afterward, they were to eat bread that was flat. It was like the bread the people had taken with them when they left Egypt. God didn't want his people ever to forget the terrible troubles he had sent to Pharaoh. God had kept sending troubles until that Egyptian king let the people of Israel go.

*For the Passover holiday, the people were to eat lamb and bread that was flat.*

Seven weeks after the Passover, there was to be a one-day Harvest Festival. The people were to thank God for sending rain and sunshine to make their crops grow. They were to thank him for the grain they had put in barns, giving them enough food for another year.

After the people of Israel arrived at their new home in Canaan, they were to celebrate the Festival of Shelters for seven days each year. During that week all the people were to move out of their houses and stay in little shelters made from tree branches. That would help them remember the forty years when they lived like that out in the lonely wilderness.

What did God want his people to remember during their Passover celebration?

What were the people to thank God for during the Harvest Festival?

Every year for the Festival of Shelters, why were God's people to live in little houses for a week?

STORY 32

# Moses Doesn't Believe God

### NUMBERS 20:1-13

During their forty years in the wilderness, God's people ran out of water several times. Each time that happened, they were upset with Moses. "Why did you make us leave Egypt?" they shouted. "We're going to die of thirst."

God told Moses and Aaron to take the shepherd's stick and gather all the people by a rock. "Speak to the rock," God said to Moses. "Then water will gush out. There will be plenty for everyone."

So Moses took his shepherd's stick and called the people together. But instead of just speaking to the rock as the Lord had told him to, Moses yelled angrily at the people. "Listen, all of you who are upset. Must we get water from the rock?" Then he hit the rock two times with his shepherd's stick, even though God had told him just to speak to it.

Suddenly water began flowing from the rock. All the people and their animals drank until they had enough. But God said, "Moses, you didn't believe me. You didn't think it would work just to speak to the rock as I told you to. So you hit it two times. The people would have seen how great I am if water had come from the rock when you only spoke to it. Now I will not let you lead my people into the Promised Land."

How sad that Moses did wrong. He had looked forward to going into the Promised Land. But now he would never be able to do that.

*Moses hit the rock two times with his shepherd's stick.*

**What did God tell Moses to do to get water?**
**What did Moses do instead?**
**What happened because Moses didn't believe God?**

# *Balaam's Donkey Speaks!*

## NUMBERS 22–24

As the Israelites continued to move toward Canaan, they came to Moab, where Balak was the king. King Balak thought the people wanted to fight with him, and he knew there were too many of them for his soldiers to win. So the king sent messengers to a man named Balaam and asked him to curse the people of Israel. To curse people means to ask God to make bad things happen to them.

The messengers told Balaam that the king would make him rich if he would curse the people of Israel. Balaam hoped that God would let him go with the messengers.

God did let Balaam go with them. "But," God said, "do only what I tell you to do." So Balaam got up early in the morning, saddled his donkey, and started off with the messengers the king had sent.

God was angry with Balaam for wanting to go with the men. So God sent an angel with a sword to stand in front of Balaam on the road. Balaam couldn't see the angel, but his donkey could. She ran into the field by the side of the road. Balaam beat his donkey and told her to behave!

The angel went farther ahead and stood in a narrow place. The donkey tried to get by but crushed Balaam's foot against a wall. Balaam beat her again.

The angel went still farther ahead and stood where there was no room to get by. The donkey lay down in the road. Once more Balaam beat her.

Then the Lord made the donkey speak like a person! She said, "What have I done to deserve getting hit by you three times?"

Balaam said she had made him look like a fool. "If I had a sword, I'd kill you," Balaam said.

The donkey asked, "Have I ever done anything like this before?"

"No," Balaam said, "you haven't."

Then the Lord helped Balaam see the angel. Balaam was afraid and threw himself on the ground in front of the angel. The angel said, "Why

*The donkey asked, "What have I done to deserve getting hit by you three times?"*

did you hit your donkey three times? I came here to stop you from doing wrong. The donkey saw me and got out of the way." Then the angel told Balaam to go on with the messengers. But he was to say only what God would tell him to say.

So Balaam went to see King Balak. The king took Balaam up on a high hill to curse the Israelites. But Balaam blessed the Israelites instead, because God told him to. This happened three times. The king was angry when Balaam blessed the Israelites. "I sent for you to curse my enemies," King Balak growled. Then he told Balaam to go home. So Balaam did.

**Why did Balaam's donkey keep stopping?**

**Have you ever heard a donkey speak?**

**What did this donkey say?**

**Why did the angel come to Balaam?**

STORY 34

# *The Promised Land*

### D E U T E R O N O M Y   3 1 ;   3 4 ;
### J O S H U A   1 : 1 – 5 : 1 2

Moses said good-bye to his people, the Israelites. He knew it was time for them to go into the Promised Land. He said that Joshua would be the new leader. Then Moses climbed to the top of a mountain and died. Since that time there has never been another leader just like Moses.

After Moses died, God said to Joshua, "Now you must lead my people. Take them across the Jordan River into the land I promised them. Be strong and brave, and be sure to obey all of my laws. Then you will always be successful. Don't be afraid, for I will be with you wherever you go."

Then Joshua sent two men across the Jordan River to check out the Promised Land around the city of Jericho. When they came to Jericho, they went into the house of a woman named Rahab. Some men from the city came there, looking for the Israelite men.

Rahab had hidden the two men on the flat roof of her house. But she told the king's messengers that the men had left the city.

That evening Rahab said to the two Israelites, "I know that the Lord has given this country to your people. Promise that you won't let any of my family be killed when Israel takes over this city."

The men promised. But they said she must keep it a secret that they had been in Jericho. Rahab warned them to hide in the nearby hills for three days until the soldiers stopped looking for them.

Rahab's house was built on the thick, high wall around the city. So she used a rope to let the two men down on the outside of the wall.

*Rahab used a rope to let the two men down on the outside of the wall.*

The men told Rahab to leave the red rope hanging from the window of her house. Then no one in her family would be hurt when the Israelite army came to take the city.

After three days the Israelite men went back across the river to tell Joshua what had happened.

Early the next morning Joshua and the people traveled to the Jordan River. Three days later Joshua said, "Tomorrow we will cross the river, and the Lord will do wonderful things among you. The priests will go first, carrying the Ark. As soon as their feet touch the water, the river will stop flowing, and they will walk through on dry ground!" (The Ark was the gold box with two gold angels on top, remember? Inside the box were the two stone tablets on which God had written the Ten Commandments.)

Everything happened just as Joshua had said. When the priests stepped into the water, it opened up in front of them. So they walked on dry ground into the middle of the river. The priests waited there while all the people walked past them into the Promised Land of Canaan.

After all the people had crossed the river, the priests followed. As soon as they stepped onto the shore on the other side, the river began flowing again!

The Israelites set up camp. And in the fields around them they found some grain, which they roasted and ate. It was the first time they had eaten anything but manna for forty years! After that, the manna stopped coming. God didn't need to send it anymore because in Canaan there was plenty of food.

........................................................................

Who became the leader of the Israelites after Moses died?

What did Rahab ask two Israelite men to do for her family in Jericho?

When the priests stepped into the Jordan River, what happened?

Why did God stop sending manna?

........................................................................

STORY 35

# Jericho's Walls Fall Down

### JOSHUA 5:13–6:27

Joshua left the Israelite camp and walked to Jericho to check out the city with its high walls. Looking up, he saw a man with a sword in his hand. Joshua went right up to him. "Are you a friend or an enemy?" he asked.

"I am in charge of the Lord's army," the man said. Joshua could tell that this was not an ordinary man. This was the Lord, who had come to help his people. So Joshua fell to the ground and worshiped him.

The people of Jericho had shut the city gates to stop the Israelites from coming in. But the Lord told Joshua how to win the fight against the city.

The Lord said, "Have all the Israelite soldiers march around the city once every day for six days. Seven priests will walk ahead of the Ark." Then God said, "Each priest will carry a ram's horn." (Did you know that a ram is a male sheep? Its horns were often used as musical horns, like trumpets.)

"On the seventh day," said the Lord, "march around Jericho, not once, but seven times. Do this while the priests blow their horns. After the seventh time around, the priests must blow a long, loud blast. When you hear this, have everyone give a mighty shout. Then the walls of the city will fall down flat, and all of my people can walk right in!"

Joshua told the people what God had said. They did as the Lord commanded.

The first day they all marched around the city once, the priests following behind the soldiers and blowing their horns. Then came the priests who carried the Ark with the Ten Commandments inside.

On the second day they marched around the city again. They did this for six days.

But on the seventh day the Israelites got up early, before it was light, and marched around the city seven times. The last time around, the priests blew a great blast on their horns. And Joshua called out to his people, "Shout, for the Lord has given you the city!"

The people gave a loud shout, and at that moment the walls of the city tumbled down. So they rushed into Jericho and took it. They saved the silver, gold, iron, and bronze for God's house. And the two men who had stayed at Rahab's house made sure that she and her family were safe.

Who talked to Joshua about how to win the fight against Jericho?

What did the people do for six days?

What happened on the seventh day?

Who in the city of Jericho was safe?

*The people gave a loud shout, and the walls of the city tumbled down.*

# Gideon and His Wool

### JUDGES 2–4; 6–8

After Joshua died, the people of Israel began worshiping idols. The Lord was very angry about this and sent armies to fight against his people.

But when God's people stopped worshiping the idols and asked the Lord for his help, he gave them leaders called judges. The judges helped them fight against their enemies and win. Yet as soon as God set the people free, they forgot him and sinned again by worshiping idols. This sinning and coming back to God went on for more than three hundred years! During that time, fifteen judges were the Israelites' leaders. One of them was a woman named Deborah. Another was a man named Gideon. This is Gideon's story.

After forty years of freedom, the people of Israel began worshiping idols again. Then the Midianites came to fight them and make slaves of them. As they had done before, the Israelites cried to the Lord for help. So the Lord sent Gideon to be their judge.

One day Gideon was threshing wheat, separating the grain from the straw. As he worked, the Lord came to him in the form of an angel.

"You will free the people of Israel from the Midianites!" the Lord told him.

"But, Lord, how can I do that?" Gideon asked.

"That's easy!" the Lord replied. "I will be with you, and you will wipe out their whole army!"

Soon a large army of Midianites came and camped nearby. Gideon blew a horn and called the men of Israel to go with him and fight them.

But first Gideon wanted God to show that he was going to help him fight the Midianites. Gideon said he would leave some wool on the ground all night. If the wool was wet with dew and the ground around it was dry in the morning, he would know that the Lord was going to help him.

*Some men lifted the water to their mouths, and some stooped down to drink.*

So Gideon left the wool on the ground all night. Early the next morning the wool was full of water, but the ground around it was dry. It was a miracle!

Then Gideon asked God to make the ground wet with dew and to let the wool stay dry. God said he would, so Gideon left the wool out another night. In the morning the wool was dry, but the ground all around it was wet. This was another miracle!

Gideon knew now that God would help him fight the Midianites. But God told Gideon that his army was too big.

"Send some of your men home," God said. "Anyone who is afraid may leave."

When Gideon told his men this, 22,000 of them went home, while 10,000 stayed.

"There are still too many!" the Lord said. "Bring them down to the river, and I will choose the ones I want in the battle."

So Gideon brought the men to the river, and they began to drink. Some lifted the water to their mouths in their hands, and some stooped down to put their mouths into the water. The Lord said that only the three hundred men who drank from their hands could go to the battle!

Gideon put those men in three groups and gave each one a horn and a clay jar with a burning torch inside. He told them that when they came to the camp of the Midianites, they must all smash their jars, blow their horns, and shout, "For the Lord and for Gideon!" That's what they did in the middle of the night.

When the Midianites heard the noise and saw the fire of the torches, they ran for their lives. The Lord made them so afraid that they even began fighting one another.

Gideon and his men chased them across the Jordan River. So the Midianites were driven out of Canaan, and the people of Israel were no longer their slaves.

- - - - - - - - - - - - - - - - - - - - - - - - - - - - - - - - - - - - - - - - - - - -

**What two miracles did God do with Gideon's wool?**

**Why did 22,000 men leave Gideon's army?**

When the men drank from the river, which ones did God send home?

How many men did God tell Gideon he could keep for the battle?

How did God help Gideon's tiny army defeat the huge Midianite army?

# Samson, the Strong Man

### JUDGES 13; 16:4-14

The people of Israel sinned again by worshiping idols. This time they became slaves to the Philistines for forty years. But a man named Manoah and his wife were among those who still worshiped the Lord.

One day the angel of the Lord came to tell Manoah's wife that she and her husband would have a son. He would be set apart for God. He was never to drink wine or any other drink like it. And he was never to have his hair cut. Someday he would free Israel from the Philistines.

When their son was born, they named him Samson. He grew up and became very strong. It was God who made him strong. But if Samson's hair was ever cut, God's power and strength would leave him.

Samson, who was Israel's judge or leader for twenty years, fell in love with a Philistine woman named Delilah. The leaders of the

*Samson easily broke the new ropes that tied him.*

Philistines told Delilah they would give her 1,100 silver coins. All she had to do was find out what made Samson strong. So Delilah begged Samson to tell her how he became strong and how he could be made as weak as other men.

Samson told her a lie. He said that if he were tied with seven wet strings from a bow, he would be as helpless as any other man.

Delilah told this to the Philistine leaders. They brought her wet strings and hid in the room. She tied Samson up while he was asleep. Then she cried out, "The Philistines are here to get you, Samson!" He woke up and broke the wet strings as easily as if they were tiny, dried-up threads.

Delilah was upset that Samson had told her a lie, so she begged him to tell her the truth. How could he be tied up so that he couldn't get away? This time Samson said that if he were tied with two new ropes that had never been used before, he would not be able to break them. So she tied him with two new ropes while men hid in the room again. As before, she called out to tell him that the Philistines were coming to get him. But he broke the new ropes too.

Delilah scolded Samson for lying to her again, and once more she begged him to tell her how to tie him so he couldn't get away. He said that if she would weave his long hair into a loom, his strength would leave him and he would be helpless. So she did this. But when she told him the Philistines were coming, Samson was as strong as ever.

What happy news did the angel of the Lord give Manoah and his wife?

When Samson grew up, who made him strong?

What would make God's strength leave Samson?

What did the Philistine leaders ask Delilah to do?

# Samson Tells a Secret

## JUDGES 16:5-6, 15-31

Delilah, the Philistine woman whom Samson had fallen in love with, turned out to be one of Samson's enemies. She tried to make Samson tell a very important secret. If he told her what made him so strong, the Philistine men would be able to take him.

Day after day Delilah begged Samson to tell her what made him strong. She gave him no rest. At last he got so tired of listening to Delilah that he told her the truth. He said that his hair had never been cut. If it were, he would no longer be strong, but as weak as other men.

Delilah could tell that Samson was finally telling the truth. She sent this message to the Philistine leaders: "Come once more. This time he has told me the truth!" So they came again and brought her the money they had promised.

Then, while Samson was asleep, one of the Philistine men cut his hair.

Delilah woke Samson up and told him that the Philistines were coming to get him. He thought he could get away as he always had before, because he didn't know that he no longer had God's strength and power. God had let his strength go away. Samson could no longer fight against the Philistines. So they tied him with heavy bronze chains. They made him blind and put him in prison, where he had to work hard grinding their corn.

While he was in prison, his hair began to grow long again. Then the Lord gave him back his strength.

One day the Philistine leaders called the people together to offer a sacrifice to their god, Dagon. Everyone praised Dagon at his temple because they thought he had helped them catch Samson.

"Send for Samson so we can tease him," someone said. So a young man led blind Samson out of prison and set him between the two pillars that held up the temple roof. Samson told the young man he wanted to put

*As Samson pushed hard, the pillars moved apart, and the roof fell.*

his hands on the pillars so he could lean against them. So the young man placed Samson's hands on the pillars.

The temple was filled with people, including all the Philistine leaders. Many of the people were having a party on the roof, laughing at Samson.

Samson prayed, "O Lord, please help me. Please make me strong one more time." He pushed against the two pillars and said, "Let me die with the Philistines." As he pushed hard, the pillars moved apart. Then the roof fell on the Philistine leaders, and all the people died.

Samson died too. But as he died, more of the enemies of Israel died with him than had died while he was alive. His family came for his body and took it back home so they could bury him near his father.

Why did Samson finally tell Delilah his secret?
What did the Philistines do to Samson then?
How did Samson use his strength when God gave it back to him?

# A Beautiful Love Story

RUTH

During the time that judges ruled Israel, a man moved his family from Israel to the land of Moab so they could have food to eat. His sons each married a young woman from Moab, and they all lived there for about ten years. Then the man and his two sons died, leaving his wife, Naomi, alone with her two daughters-in-law.

Naomi wanted to go back home to the city of Bethlehem in Israel. Her daughters-in-law started the trip with her. When she told them they should go back to their own homes, they cried. One of them, Orpah, went back to Moab. But Ruth didn't want to leave Naomi.

"I'll go with you," Ruth said, "and live wherever you live. Your friends will be my friends, and your God will be my God."

So Naomi let Ruth come with her to Bethlehem.

One day Ruth said to Naomi, "Let me go out to the fields. I will pick up grain dropped by the workers." She knew that one of God's laws said that people with fields were to let poor people pick up any grain that the field workers left. They could take this home to make food.

Naomi said Ruth could go to the fields. So Ruth found a field belonging to a man named Boaz and began picking up the grain that his workers left. When Boaz came out to the field later that morning, he asked the man in charge, "Who is that young woman over there?"

"She is the one who came with Naomi from the land of Moab," the man replied.

Boaz went over and talked to Ruth. He was kind and told her to stay with his workers. When she was thirsty, he said she should help herself to as much water as she wanted. And he told her to sit with his workers and eat the lunch he put out for them.

Ruth thanked him and asked him why he was so kind to her. Boaz said it was because he knew about her kindness to her mother-in-law. He knew that she had left her family and the land where she was born. She had come to live among the people of Israel to worship God.

Ruth stayed in the field until evening. Then she took the grain she had gathered and carried it home to her mother-in-law. Naomi was happy to see how much Ruth brought. She asked Ruth who had let her pick the grain.

Ruth said, "The man's name is Boaz." Naomi was surprised because he was from her husband's family!

Ruth went back day after day until the grain was all gathered.

One day Naomi said to Ruth, "Boaz will be working with the grain tonight." She told Ruth to find Boaz, and she told her what to say to him.

Boaz worked hard that night. After a big supper, he lay down for the night beside a pile of grain. When it was dark, Ruth went over and lay at his feet. Around midnight he woke up, surprised that someone was there. "Who is it?" he asked.

"It's only me, sir," Ruth replied. Then she said what Naomi had told her to say. Because he was from Naomi's husband's family, Ruth said she wanted him to marry her and take care of her.

*Ruth picked up the grain that the workers left.*

The idea pleased him very much. "May the Lord bless you, my child," he replied. He said he would gladly marry her, if he could, but first he needed to make sure it was all right with another man in Naomi's family.

The next day Boaz talked with the man, and he told Boaz to marry Ruth. Soon ten city leaders in Bethlehem learned about it. All of them prayed that the Lord would bless Ruth and Boaz.

Naomi was happy when Boaz married Ruth. She was even happier when the Lord gave them a son. They named the baby Obed, and they loved him very much. So did his grandmother, Naomi!

Why didn't Ruth want to stay in Moab?

Why did Ruth go out to a field?

How did Boaz show that he was kind?

What did God do for Ruth and Boaz after they got married?

STORY 40

# *Job Goes Through Sad Times*

JOB 1–19

There was a man in the land of Uz named Job, who worshiped God and always did what was good and right. God gave him seven sons and three daughters. And he had 7,000 sheep, 3,000 camels, 1,000 oxen, 500 donkeys, and many servants. His animals were worth a lot of money. In fact, he was the richest man in that part of the world.

After many years, God let all of Job's animals and children be taken from him. God let this happen to see if Job would still love and worship him.

Job said, "I had nothing of my own when I was born, and I will have nothing when I die. It was God who gave me my children and everything else I had. And now it is God who has taken them all away. He knows what is best, and I thank him for being the great God that he is."

To test Job
even more, God let
him be covered with sores.
Job's wife became angry. She said,
"Why do you still trust God? Speak against him
for treating you like this."

Job answered her, "You are talking like a foolish
woman. After God has given us so many good things,
should we not accept bad things too?"

So Job still said nothing that was wrong.

Three friends came to comfort Job. They cried and
sat beside him on the ground. They said nothing for
many days because they could see how bad he felt.

These friends thought Job's troubles had been sent
to him because he had done things that were wrong. After a while they
said, "You must have sinned. But if you will be sorry for your sins, God
will forgive you and make you well again."

Job knew he had not done anything wrong. He said to them, "You
came to help me feel better, but your words don't help me at all. I wish
you hadn't come."

Then Job said, "I wish that God would let me die so that I wouldn't
need to go through such sad times anymore! Oh, that I had someone to
speak to God for me, for he doesn't listen to my prayers anymore. Yet I
know that my Savior is alive, and that after many years he will come to
earth. And someday I shall rise from the grave and see God for myself."

......................................................................................

**What sad things did God let happen to Job?**

**Why did God let these things happen?**

**What did Job's friends say that upset him?**

**Whom would Job see someday?**

......................................................................................

# God Speaks to Job

## JOB 20-42

When Job could neither die nor get well, he became upset. He began to say that his troubles were too great and that God was being unkind to him.

Instead of trying to cheer up Job, his three friends kept telling him he must have been very bad to have so much pain. Job became angry with his friends, and they became angry with him. They kept on talking back and forth for a long time, and all of them said things they shouldn't have.

Then God spoke through the wind. He reminded Job that he had made the earth, the sea, and the sky. God made it clear that he is the one who gives the wild animals their food and feeds the young birds when they are hungry. It is God who gives the beautiful tail to the peacock and the feathers to the ostrich. He makes the horse fast and strong and brave. He teaches the eagle to build her nest on the high rocks and to find food for her young ones.

After God spoke, Job knew he had sinned when he said that God was unkind. "I have spoken of things that I don't understand. I am sorry for my sin, and I sit here in the dust to show how sorry I am."

After this the Lord made Job well again. God blessed Job two times as much as before. Now Job had 14,000 sheep, 6,000 camels, 2,000 oxen, and 1,000 donkeys. He also had seven more sons and

*Job had two times as many children as before.*

three more daughters. So now, counting those already in heaven, he had two times as many children as before.

Job lived 140 years more after all these things happened to him. And he died when he was a very old man.

What were some things God reminded Job about?

How did Job show he was sorry for saying God was unkind?

What good things did God do for Job after all of his sad times?

STORY 42

# *Jonah and the Giant Fish*

## JONAH

Long ago Nineveh was one of the greatest cities in the world, but it was also a very wicked city.

One day God said to the prophet Jonah, "Go to Nineveh. Tell the people that I am going to punish them because of their sins."

But Jonah didn't want to go. Instead, he ran away to Joppa, a city by the sea. There he found a ship headed in the opposite direction from Nineveh. So Jonah bought a ticket and got on board to try to get away from God.

After the ship sailed out to sea, the Lord sent a strong wind. The ship was in danger of sinking. But Jonah had gone to sleep at the bottom of the ship. The captain found him and woke him up.

"How can you sleep like this?" the captain shouted. "Get up and pray to your God. Perhaps he will help us so we won't die."

Then the sailors said to one another, "This storm has been sent because someone on the ship has done something wrong. Let's draw straws to find out who it is."

They did, and Jonah drew the short one. They said to him, "Tell us, what wicked thing have you done? What country do you come from?"

*The fish spit Jonah out on the shore.*

Jonah replied, "I am from Israel, and I am running away from the God who made the sea and the land."

Then the men were afraid and asked, "What should we do so that the storm will stop?"

Jonah told them, "If you throw me into the sea, it will become still again. I know that the storm is my fault."

The sailors didn't want to do it. But they knew they had to. As soon as they threw Jonah into the water, the wind stopped and the sea was still. The men were amazed. They worshiped God and promised to obey him.

The Lord sent a huge fish to swallow Jonah as soon as he was thrown into the water! Jonah stayed alive in the fish three days and three nights. He told God he was sorry about his sin. God heard his prayer and told the fish to spit him out on the shore.

Then God spoke to Jonah a second time. "Go to Nineveh," he said, "and give the people there my message."

So Jonah went to Nineveh. There he shouted out God's message. "In forty days Nineveh will be destroyed because of the sins of its people."

When the king of Nineveh and his people heard this, they believed that God had sent Jonah, and they believed what he said would come true. They stopped doing things that were wrong and started praying to God.

God knew that the people were sorry. So he did not destroy the city after all.

Jonah was very angry about this, because the people of Nineveh were enemies of Israel. Jonah was also afraid that people would laugh at him and say he didn't know what he was talking about.

He said to the Lord, "I knew you wouldn't destroy the city. That's why I ran away. Now I would rather die than live."

Jonah went to a place outside the city and waited to see if God would destroy it. That night the Lord caused a vine to grow, and the next day its thick leaves shaded Jonah's head from the hot sun. He was very glad it was there. But soon God sent a worm that ate through the stem, and the vine died. Then God sent a hot wind, and the sun beat down on Jonah. He grew tired and sick from the heat. Again he became angry.

Then God said, "You are angry because I have destroyed the vine, but you want me to destroy Nineveh. That's a city with more than 120,000 people who don't know the right way to live! Shouldn't I care about them?"

So God taught Jonah how wrong he was to wish that Nineveh would be destroyed.

How did Jonah try to get away from God?

How did God save Jonah when sailors threw him overboard?

Why was Jonah angry that the people of Nineveh were sorry for their sins?

What did God plant to teach Jonah not to be upset?

STORY 43

# Samuel Hears a Voice

### 1 SAMUEL 1–3

Hannah and her husband went to the Tabernacle in Shiloh every year to worship God.

Hannah was unhappy because she had no children. So one day while Hannah was at the Tabernacle, she prayed for a son. She promised that her child would serve God all his life.

Eli the priest saw Hannah's lips moving. But he couldn't hear her speaking. He thought she was drunk.

Hannah told him, "Oh no, sir, I am not drunk. I am praying with all my heart." Eli told her he hoped God would give her what she prayed for.

God answered Hannah's prayer and gave her a son. She named him Samuel, which means "I asked the Lord for him."

*Samuel stayed at the Tabernacle and helped Eli.*

*Samuel said, "Speak, Lord.
I am listening."*

When Samuel was old enough to live at the Tabernacle, Hannah and her husband took him there. They took him to help the priests with God's work.

"Do you remember me?" Hannah asked Eli. "I prayed for this child several years ago. As long as he lives, he will belong to the Lord." So Hannah and her husband let Samuel stay at the Tabernacle to help Eli the priest.

Eli's two sons were also priests. God said that his priests must be holy and do what is right. But Eli's sons did things that were wrong. And Eli didn't make his sons stop being priests, as he should have done.

Samuel did what was right and pleasing to the Lord. His mother made him a coat each year and brought it to him when she and her husband came to the Tabernacle to worship God.

Samuel stayed at the Tabernacle and helped Eli.

One night after Samuel went to bed, he heard a voice calling him. "I'm here," he answered. He jumped up and ran to ask Eli what he wanted.

But Eli said, "I didn't call you. Go back to bed."

When Samuel lay down, he heard the voice again. He ran to Eli and asked, "Why are you calling me, Eli?"

"I didn't call you, my son," Eli said. "Go and lie down."

So Samuel lay down again. But he heard the voice a third time. He went to Eli and said, "I'm sure I heard you calling me. What do you want me to do?"

Then Eli knew it was God who had called the child. He said to Samuel, "Go lie down. If you hear a voice again, say, 'Speak, Lord. I am listening.'"

So Samuel went back to bed. The Lord called as before, "Samuel, Samuel."

Samuel answered, "Speak, Lord. I am listening." Then the Lord told him he was going to punish Eli and his sons. God said that Eli's sons were wicked, and Eli hadn't punished them.

The next day Samuel told Eli what God had said. Eli knew that everything Samuel said was true.

As Samuel grew up, he kept on listening to God. And he told the people of Israel what God wanted them to know.

What did Hannah ask God to give her?
Why did Hannah and her husband take Samuel to the Tabernacle?
How many times did Samuel think Eli was calling him one night?
What did Samuel say the fourth time God called him?
What did the Lord tell Samuel?

# The People Want a King

### 1 SAMUEL 7–10

When Samuel grew up, God chose him to be the new judge of Israel.

Samuel said to his people, "If you will get rid of your idols and obey the Lord, he will save you from the Philistines." So the people got rid of their idols. Then Samuel told them, "Come, all of you, to the city of Mizpah, and I will pray for you."

When the Philistines heard that the people were at Mizpah, they went to fight them there. The Israelites were afraid and said to Samuel, "Pray

*Saul was good looking and taller than anyone else in Israel.*

hard that God will save us." Samuel took a young lamb and gave it as an offering to the Lord. Then Samuel prayed, and the Lord listened to him. As the Philistine army came closer, God spoke with the sound of thunder. Then they ran away in fear.

When Samuel was old, the leaders of Israel told him they wanted a king so that they would be like the other nations around them. God said to Samuel, "The people don't want me to be their king any longer. You may do what they ask, but warn them what it will be like to have a king."

So Samuel told them, "The king will make your sons serve in his army and work in his fields. Your daughters will be cooks and bakers in his kitchen. He will steal the best of your fields and gardens, and he will take your cattle and sheep. When you cry out because of the trouble your king will bring to you, God won't help you."

But the people still wanted a king.

A young man named Saul was good looking and taller than anyone else in Israel. One day some donkeys that belonged to Saul's father ran away. Saul's father said to him, "Take a servant with you, and look for the donkeys."

Saul and the servant couldn't find the donkeys. Finally Saul said, "Let's go back. By now my father has probably stopped worrying about the donkeys and is worrying about us!"

They were near the city where Samuel lived. So the servant told Saul that a prophet lived there. "Let's go ask him to find the donkeys."

"That's a good idea," Saul replied.

Saul found Samuel, the prophet. The Lord had already told Samuel, "Today I will send you the man who will be king of Israel." Now the Lord said to Samuel, "This is the man I told you about."

Samuel asked Saul to come to a special dinner. As for the donkeys, Samuel said that Saul's father had already found them!

Samuel gave Saul and his servant the best places to sit at the dinner. Then Samuel asked them to stay for the night.

The next morning, Samuel took a bottle of olive oil and poured it on Saul's head. This meant that God had chosen Saul to be the king of Israel.

One day not long afterward, Samuel told the people that Saul would be their king. Everyone wanted to see Saul, but he was hiding! The Lord told the people where to look, and they found him.

Saul was a big, handsome fellow, taller than any of the rest of them. Samuel said, "Here is the man God has chosen to be your king."

And the people shouted, "Long live the king!"

Why did the people of Israel want a king?

What troubles did Samuel say a king would bring?

How did Samuel show Saul that God had chosen him to be king?

Find Saul, the tallest man in the picture on page 94. What did the people shout when they saw him?

STORY 45

# A New King

1 SAMUEL 15–16; 17:34-36

Sometimes King Saul obeyed God. But he did not always do everything God told him.

One day God told Samuel, "I am sorry that I let Saul be king. He has not obeyed me."

Samuel felt sad. He knew he had to give King Saul some bad news. When he found the king, Samuel told him, "You have not obeyed God. So he will not let you keep on being the king."

Then God talked to Samuel again. He told Samuel to find a man in Bethlehem named Jesse. God said to anoint one of Jesse's sons by pouring oil on his head. That would set him apart as the next king.

The Lord told Samuel, "I will show you which son to anoint."

As God commanded, Samuel went to Bethlehem. He saw that Jesse's oldest son was a fine-looking young man. Samuel thought God would want

*David protected his sheep from the lion.*

him to be the next king. But the Lord said no. He said, "Don't choose a person by the way he looks. I don't choose people that way. I see their thoughts and know what is in their hearts."

Then Jesse called his second son, but the Lord said no. Jesse brought out his third, fourth, fifth, sixth, and seventh sons. But Samuel said, "The Lord has not chosen any of these. Are these all the sons you have?"

"No," Jesse answered. "There is one other. My youngest son is out taking care of the sheep."

David often watched his father's sheep. One time a lion grabbed a lamb. David went after the lion and hit it with a club. Then the lion dropped the lamb and came after David. But David caught the lion by the part of its mane that came down around its chin and killed it. Another time David used his hands to kill a bear.

"Send for your youngest son," Samuel said. So Jesse had David brought in from the fields.

The Lord said to Samuel, "Anoint him, for this is the one." So Samuel poured oil on David's head. Then the Lord sent his Holy Spirit into David's heart to make him wise and good. But the Lord took his Spirit away from Saul.

Good spirits, like angels, serve God. Evil spirits serve Satan. One of these evil spirits went into Saul to make him afraid and angry. Saul's helpers suggested that harp music might chase out the evil spirit whenever it troubled him.

One of Saul's men knew that David could play the harp well. So King Saul sent messengers to Jesse and told him to send his son David to the king. Jesse got a young goat and loaded a donkey with bread and wine. He sent these with David as a present to King Saul.

David stayed with Saul and helped him. Whenever the evil spirit troubled Saul, David played soft music on a harp. Then the evil spirit would go away. When Saul felt better, David would return home. He would take care of his father's sheep until the next time the king needed him.

Why wouldn't God let Saul keep on being king?

Why didn't Samuel choose Jesse's oldest son to be the next king?

Before David took Saul's job as king, how did David help King Saul?

# David Kills a Giant

## 1 SAMUEL 17

The Philistine army was coming to fight Israel. So King Saul and the Israelite army got ready for the battle.

One of the Philistine soldiers was a giant named Goliath. He wore a lot of heavy armor. He had a bronze helmet to protect his head. He wore a hard metal coat. And sheets of bronze covered his legs so that no sword or spear could hurt him.

Goliath stood in the valley between the two armies and yelled to the army of Israel, "I'll fight the best man in your army. If he can kill me, we Philistines will be your slaves. But if I kill him, then you must be our slaves!"

The Israelite men in Saul's army were afraid to fight with the giant. For forty days he came out every morning and evening to dare the men of Israel to fight him.

David's three oldest brothers were in Saul's army, but David was at home taking care of his father's sheep. One day David's father said to him, "Take this food to your brothers, and take this cheese to their captain. See how they are getting along."

David found his brothers. As he was talking to them, Goliath came out and shouted at the Israelites the way he always did.

"How dare this giant talk like that to the army of the living God!" David said. When some of the men saw that David wanted to fight Goliath, they told Saul. So the king sent for him.

"You can't fight that giant," Saul said. "Why, you're only a boy, and Goliath has been a soldier for many years."

"But I can!" David answered. "I have kept my father's sheep safe by getting rid of a lion and a bear with my hands. I'll get rid of this wicked giant, too. The Lord who saved me from the lion and the bear will save me from the giant."

"All right," Saul said. "Go and fight him, and the Lord be with you."

Then Saul gave David his bronze helmet and metal coat. But David said, "I'm not used to these." So he took them off.

The young shepherd took only a sling and the stick that he used to keep the sheep safe. Choosing five smooth stones from a stream of water, he put them into his shepherd's bag.

*David sent the stone sailing toward Goliath.*

Then he walked toward Goliath.

The giant didn't think David was worth fighting. He was just a shepherd boy. "Come over here so I can kill you," Goliath yelled.

David answered, "You come to me trusting in your sword, your shield, and your spear. But I come to you trusting in the God of Israel. Today he will help me win!"

As Goliath came closer, David ran toward him. Reaching into his shepherd's bag, he took out a stone, put it into his sling, and sent it sailing toward Goliath. It hit the giant right in the forehead, and he fell to the ground. He never got up again.

The Philistines began running away. Then the army of Israel started after them. The Israelites won against their enemy.

---

**Who was Goliath?**

**Why did David believe he could fight Goliath and win?**

**What did David use to fight Goliath?**

**Tell about David's fight with the giant.**

---

STORY 47

# *David's Best Friend*

## 1 SAMUEL 18:1-16; 19:1-10; 20

After he won the fight with Goliath, David talked to King Saul. Then he met the king's son Jonathan. The two young men became best friends. From that day, David lived at Saul's palace. Jonathan gave David his robe and shirt and belt. He also gave David his sword and his bow for shooting arrows.

Saul made David a captain in his army. But King Saul soon became jealous of David because people praised David more than Saul.

Saul was so angry that he wanted David to be killed. But Jonathan begged his father not to hurt David. He said, "David killed Goliath. Then we won against the Philistines. You were happy then, so why are you trying to kill David now?"

Saul promised not to hurt David. So David played the harp for the king as before.

But an evil spirit came into Saul's heart. While David was playing the harp, Saul threw his spear at David, who jumped away just in time. Then David ran for his life.

Jonathan promised David he would do everything he could to help.

*David and Jonathan became best friends.*

The next day was a special religious holiday, and Saul expected David to eat at his table. But David was afraid to go. He said to Jonathan, "Tell your father that I asked to go home to Bethlehem. If Saul is angry when he hears this, we'll know that he wants to kill me. But if he isn't angry, we'll know everything is all right." Jonathan agreed to this plan.

"But how will I find out what your father says?" David asked Jonathan.

"Come out into the field with me," Jonathan said. He showed David a large rock and told him to hide behind it. "I will come out here the day after tomorrow and shoot three arrows," said Jonathan. "And I'll send a boy to pick them up. If I tell him that the arrows are on this side, you will know that my father is not angry. But if I say that the arrows are ahead of him, then you must leave so my father can't hurt you."

When David's seat at Saul's table was empty for two days, Saul asked Jonathan, "Where is David?"

Jonathan answered, "David asked if he could go to Bethlehem to be with his family."

Saul was angry with Jonathan. He said, "You'll never get to be king as long as David is alive. Bring him to me so I can kill him."

The next day Jonathan went to the field where David was hiding. He took a boy with him. Then he shot an arrow over the boy's head.

"The arrow is ahead of you. Go find it. Hurry," Jonathan shouted to him. Then David knew he must go away.

Jonathan gave his bow and arrows to the boy with him. He told the boy to take them back to the city.

David came out from his hiding place. The two friends cried together. Jonathan told David to go in peace. He said they would always be friends. So David had to run away and keep hiding, but he had done nothing wrong.

Who became David's best friend?

What did Saul do with his spear?

What did it mean when Jonathan shot an arrow past the boy with him?

What did David and Jonathan promise each other?

# David Steals the King's Spear

### 1 SAMUEL 23:13; 24:8-17; 26–27

David had to go from one place to another to hide from King Saul. Soon about six hundred men were traveling with David. One time the king came into a cave where David was hiding. The king didn't see him, but David got close enough to cut off part of the king's robe. David could have killed the king, but he didn't. When David called out to King Saul and told him what he had done, the king began to cry. He said to David, "You are a better man than I am. You have done good to me, while I have done wrong to you." Then Saul went back home.

But Saul still wanted to kill David. Sometime later, when some of David's enemies told King Saul where David was hiding, he took three thousand men to look for him.

David heard about it and sent some of his men to see what Saul was doing. They soon brought back word that Saul had come. Then David and another man quietly went into Saul's camp one night. Saul was sleeping, and his spear was stuck in the ground by his head. Abner, the general of Saul's army, and the rest of his soldiers were sleeping around the king.

The man with David wanted to kill Saul. But David said no. "Don't do it," he said. "It would be a sin to kill the king God gave us. Perhaps he will die in a battle. But I won't kill him."

Then David had an idea. He said to his friend, "Let's steal his spear and bottle of water!" So they crawled up close to Saul's head and took the spear and water. They got away before anyone woke up, because the Lord had put Saul and his men into a deep sleep.

Then David stood on top of a hill where he was safe and shouted to Abner. Saul's general woke up suddenly and jumped to his feet. "Who is it?" he called.

David shouted back, "Why haven't you watched over the king better, so that no one could come and kill him? Where are the king's spear and the bottle of water that were beside his head?"

*David quietly took Saul's spear and water bottle.*

By now Saul was awake. He knew David's voice but asked, "Is that you, David?"

David said, "Yes, my king. Why are you still chasing me and trying to kill me?"

Saul said, "I have sinned. I have been wrong. Come back, my son, for I won't try to hurt you anymore."

David answered, "Here is your spear. Let one of the young men with you come over and get it."

Then David left, and Saul went back home.

David didn't believe that Saul would stop trying to kill him. The king had cried and called David his son before.

"Someday he will finally find me and kill me," David said to himself. "I must go and live in the land of the Philistines. Then Saul will give up looking for me."

So David took his men and their families to a Philistine city. The king there welcomed David and all the others, letting them stay in his land. Then he gave them the city of Ziklag to live in. He hoped David and his men would help his people in times of war.

When Saul heard that David had gone to live with the Philistines, he stopped looking for him.

----

**What did David say when the man with him wanted to kill King Saul?**

**What did David do instead of killing the king?**

**Where did David go to live so that Saul would stop looking for him?**

# David Becomes the King

## 1 SAMUEL 31; 2 SAMUEL 1–2; 4–5

While David was living in Ziklag in the land of the Philistines, those people began fighting King Saul. One day Saul and his army lost the battle with the Philistines, and the Philistine soldiers began moving in on the king. They killed Jonathan and two of Saul's other sons. Then Saul fell on his own sword and died.

Soon a messenger arrived in Ziklag to tell David about it. "The Israelites have lost the battle and many are dead. Saul and Jonathan are dead too."

David cried for Saul and his son Jonathan, and for all the men of Israel who had died. Then David asked the Lord if he should go to the land of Israel. And God said yes. David asked God where in Israel he should go. And the Lord told him, "Go to the city of Hebron."

David was now thirty years old. When he came to Hebron, the leaders of the tribe of Judah asked him to be their king, and he agreed. He must have been thinking about the day many years before, when he was a teenage boy and Samuel had anointed his head with oil. David knew that God had chosen him to be the next king.

Now the time had come for David to be the new ruler of God's people, the Israelites. But at first, only the tribe of Judah made him their king. The other tribes of Israel didn't

*Samuel anointed David's head with oil.*

107

come to David, for they already had a king. He was a son of Saul. But one day two captains from that king's army killed him.

When the other tribes saw that their king was dead, they asked David to be their king. So at last David was king over all twelve of the tribes of Israel.

David now took over the city of Jerusalem and lived there in a strong fort. He became a very great man, for the Lord helped him in everything he did.

King Hiram of Tyre and King David were good friends. King Hiram's people were very good builders. So Hiram sent men to build a palace for David in Jerusalem.

---

When Saul and his army lost to the Philistines, why did David cry?

Which tribe of Israel made David their king first?

How many of the twelve tribes of Israel finally made David their king?

Where did David build his palace?

---

STORY 50

# God's Beautiful Temple

## 2 SAMUEL 7; 1 KINGS 3; 5–7; 1 CHRONICLES 22; 2 CHRONICLES 1:1–5:6

David loved God and always tried to do what was right. But sometimes he did things that were very wrong. Then he let God know how sorry he was. God loved David and always forgave him.

David wanted to build the Temple. It would be a special building where God would live and his people would worship him. But God said no. God wanted David's son Solomon to build the Temple.

Solomon loved God. He always tried to do what was right, just like David, his father. After David died, Solomon became the new king.

One night God spoke to King Solomon in a dream, telling him he could have anything he wanted! Solomon asked for wisdom. He wanted to know about everything and understand everything. He always wanted to know the best way to help his people.

God was pleased that Solomon had not asked to have a lot of money or a long life, or to win when he fought his enemies. Because Solomon hadn't done that, God would give him the wisdom he asked for and all these other things too!

Solomon asked his father's friend, King Hiram of Tyre, to send wood so he could build the Temple. So Hiram's men cut down cedar trees and brought them to the sea. There they made them into rafts and floated them toward Jerusalem.

Solomon carefully followed the pattern his father, David, had given him. When the walls were up, Solomon placed cedar boards on the inside of the walls. These boards were carved with the shapes of flowers and covered with gold. Even the floor of the Temple was covered with gold.

Across the middle of the Temple he hung a blue, purple, and red curtain. This made two rooms just as there had been in the Tabernacle. The room at the back was for the Ark and was called the Most Holy Place. In this special room he made two figures of angels with their wings spread out. The figures were fifteen feet high. They were carved from the wood of olive trees and covered with gold. Their wings reached from one side of the little room to the other.

Solomon asked for one of Hiram's best workers to come and make the Temple as beautiful and perfect as possible. This man made beautiful things from gold, silver, bronze, and iron. He also made things from wood and from fine linen cloth.

He made two great bronze pillars to stand in front of the Temple. And he made a bronze altar, which was four times as large as the one Moses had made for the Tabernacle. A great tank of water rested on the backs of twelve bronze oxen.

He made ten brass tubs set on wheels so they could be moved from one place to another. These would hold water for washing sacrifices to be offered to God.

*The people brought animals to sacrifice as gifts to God.*

And he made ten gold lampstands to give light inside the Temple.

It took seven years to finish all this work! Then God's people brought lambs, goats, and cattle to be sacrificed as gifts to God.

What did Solomon ask for when God promised to give him anything he
wanted?

What might you ask for if you could have just one wish?

What were some things God gave Solomon even though he didn't ask
for them?

How did King Hiram help Solomon?

Name two or three things that were used to make the Temple beautiful.

STORY 51

# Two Kings and Two Kingdoms

### 1 KINGS 11:41–12:20; 2 CHRONICLES 10–11

Solomon was the king of Israel for forty years. Then he died and was buried in Jerusalem.

After that, the people went to talk with Solomon's son Rehoboam. The people told him how hard his father, Solomon, was on them when he was their king. If Rehoboam promised to treat them better than his father had, they would let him be their king.

Rehoboam told them to come back in three days. At that time he would give them his answer.

After they had gone, Rehoboam went to the old men who had been friends of his father. He asked them how he should treat the people. They told him to be kind to the people. If he was kind, everyone would be happy to let him be king for as long as he lived.

But Rehoboam did not like what the old men said. So he asked the young men who had grown up with him what they thought. The young men told him to be even harder on the people than his father had been.

When the people came back for his answer three days later, Rehoboam followed the advice of the young men. He shouted, "If you think my father was hard on you, well, I'll be even harder on you than he was."

The people were angry. Only the tribes of Judah and Benjamin let Rehoboam be their king. The other ten tribes said he could not be their king. They wanted Jeroboam instead.

So now there were two kings ruling over God's people. Rehoboam, Solomon's son, was king over just two tribes in the south. His kingdom was called Judah. Jeroboam was king over the other ten tribes in the north. His kingdom was called Israel.

One day King Jeroboam said to himself, "My people will want to worship at the Temple. That's in the city of Jerusalem, which is in Judah. There they will see King Rehoboam, son of the great King Solomon. And they will want him to be their king instead of me."

So King Jeroboam made two gold idols shaped like calves. He put them in different parts of Israel—one at Bethel and the other at Dan. The people went there to worship the idols. They went because Jeroboam said to the people, "It is too far for you to go to Jerusalem to worship God. These gold idols are your gods. Worship them." What a wicked thing for Jeroboam to say!

All the good priests who lived in Israel moved to Jerusalem in Judah.

*The people of Israel worshiped gold idols shaped like calves.*

And many other good people who would not worship the gold calves went with them. They chose Rehoboam as their king.

What did Rehoboam say that made the people angry?

Which were the only two tribes that let Rehoboam, Solomon's son, be their king?

What wicked thing did Jeroboam do after he became king of the northern ten tribes of Israel?

Where did the good people from Israel move?

# *Food for Elijah*

## 1 KINGS 15–18

Jeroboam was a bad king, but he ruled over the ten tribes of Israel for twenty-two years. The kings who ruled after he died were bad too. King Ahab was worse than any of the others.

Ahab married the daughter of a king who did not worship God. The woman's name was Jezebel, and she worshiped Baal, a god that was not real.

King Ahab worshiped Baal too. The Lord was angry with King Ahab and sent the prophet Elijah to him. Elijah told Ahab that God would keep it from raining in the land of Israel for many years. God would not send rain until Elijah asked him to send it.

The Lord told Elijah to hide after he talked to the king. "Hide beside a brook east of the Jordan River," the Lord said. "You can drink water from the brook, and I have told the birds to feed you!" So Elijah hid by the brook. Big, black birds called ravens brought him food every morning and evening, just as God promised. But after a while the brook dried up because there had been no rain.

Then the Lord said to Elijah, "Go to the city of Zarephath. I have told a woman who lives there to feed you."

When Elijah came to the gate of the city, he saw a woman gathering sticks. He called to her, "Please bring me a cup of water." As she was going to get it, he called to her again. "And bring a piece of bread, too!"

But she answered, "God knows I have no bread. I have only a handful of flour in a jar and a little olive oil in a bottle. Now I am gathering sticks for a fire so I can bake a small loaf of bread for my son and me. After we eat it, we will have no more food and we will die."

But Elijah said, "No, you won't. Bake the bread, but make a small loaf for me first. Then there will be plenty left for you and your son. That's because the Lord says the little flour and olive oil you have will last until he sends rain and the crops grow again."

The woman did as Elijah said. And sure enough, there was always olive oil left in the bottle and flour in the jar, no matter how much she used! It was a wonderful miracle that continued for as long as there was no rain.

During this time, King Ahab was becoming more and more upset. It was so dry that there wasn't even enough grass for his horses and mules to eat. Elijah told him that there was no rain because the king and his family would not obey God.

Then Elijah, God's prophet, won a contest with 450 prophets who worshiped Baal. After that, Elijah told Ahab a rainstorm would come soon.

Elijah prayed, and before long there was a little cloud in the sky. Then there were big, black clouds. The wind began to blow hard. And God answered Elijah's prayer by sending a rainstorm. Once again the crops could grow, and no one would be hungry!

.................................................................................

Why was God angry with King Ahab?

What did Elijah tell Ahab?

How did God feed Elijah while he was hiding beside a brook?

How did a woman with just a little flour and oil help Elijah?

What was God's answer to Elijah's prayer for rain?

.................................................................................

*Ravens brought Elijah food just as God promised.*

*A chariot of fire pulled by horses of fire took Elijah away.*

# A Chariot Ride to Heaven

## 1 KINGS 19; 2 KINGS 2

As God's prophet, Elijah taught people about God and brought them messages from God. He felt sad when people didn't believe him and when they worshiped Baal instead of God. But the Lord God let Elijah know there were many people who did not worship Baal.

Then God told Elijah to find the man who would soon take his place. That man was a farmer named Elisha. Soon the two men began traveling together.

When the Lord was ready to take Elijah up to heaven, Elijah wanted to be alone. So he said to Elisha, "Stay here, please, for the Lord has told me to go to Bethel."

But Elisha said, "I'll never leave you." So they went to Bethel together.

Then Elijah said to Elisha, "Stay here at Bethel, please, for the Lord has told me to go to Jericho."

But Elisha said, "I'll never leave you." So they went to Jericho.

Then Elijah said to Elisha, "Stay here at Jericho, for the Lord has told me to go to the Jordan River."

But again Elisha answered, "I'll never leave you." So they went on together.

At the river, Elijah hit the water with his coat. Then the river divided into two parts so he and Elisha could walk across on dry ground!

When they were on the other side, Elijah said to Elisha, "Tell me what you want me to do for you before I am taken away."

Elisha asked to have even more of God's Spirit upon him than Elijah had.

"You have asked a hard thing," Elijah said. "But if you see me when I am taken from you, then you will receive what you are asking for."

As they walked along, suddenly a chariot of fire pulled by horses of fire came between the two men and took Elijah away. Then a wind came, spinning round and round. It took Elijah up to heaven in the chariot. Elisha saw it and cried out, "My father, my father, I see the chariot and its drivers!"

Elisha never saw Elijah again on earth. He picked up Elijah's coat from the ground and hit the river with it. Then the water divided into two parts as it had for Elijah, and Elisha went across on dry ground!

One day the leaders of Jericho told Elisha, "Our city is beautiful, but the water is no good. Nothing will grow here."

"Bring me a new bowl with salt in it," Elisha told them. So they did. He went to the spring where the city got its water and threw the salt into it. He said, "The Lord has made the water good. It will never hurt anyone or keep the crops from growing." And sure enough, the water was always good after that.

Whom did God choose to take Elijah's place?

What did Elisha ask Elijah to do before he left this earth?

How was Elijah taken to heaven?

What did Elisha do to the water of Jericho?

STORY 54

# Elisha Helps a Rich Woman

## 2 KINGS 4:8-37

As Elisha was traveling around the land, he came to the city of Shunem. A rich woman who lived there asked him to stop at her house for dinner. From then on, whenever he came that way, he stopped for a meal.

One day the woman said to her husband, "I'm sure this man is a prophet of the Lord. Let's make a little room for him. Whenever he comes to visit us, it will be ready for him." So that is what they did.

Once when Elisha was there with his servant, Gehazi, the two men said to the woman, "You have been very kind to us. What can we do for you?" But she said she didn't need anything.

Later Elisha asked Gehazi, "Can you think of anything we can do for her?"

Gehazi said, "She has no child."

Then Elisha told the kind woman that the Lord would give her a son. And Elisha's words came true the following year.

When the child was old enough, he went out to the field with his father. While he was there, he cried out, "My head! Oh, my head!"

His father said to one of the servants, "Carry him to his mother." The child sat in his mother's lap until noon, and then he died.

*How thankful the child's mother was that her son was alive.*

The sad woman took her son up to Elisha's room and laid him on the bed. Then she sent a message to her husband in the field, asking him for a servant and a donkey. She said she wanted to visit the prophet. But she didn't tell her husband that their boy was dead.

When the woman and the servant came to Mount Carmel, Elisha saw them. He said to Gehazi, "Run to meet the woman from Shunem. Ask her if everything is all right."

Gehazi ran to ask her. And she said, "Everything is fine." But when she came to Elisha, she took hold of his feet. She told him, "You said I would have a son. But I shouldn't have gotten my hopes up." Then Elisha knew that her boy was dead.

Elisha went home with the woman. He went to his room, where the boy was on the bed. Elisha shut the door and prayed. Then he put his mouth on the child's mouth. He put his eyes on the child's eyes and his hands on the child's hands. And the child's body became warm again!

Elisha walked around the room for a while. Then he came back to the child. This time the boy sneezed seven times, opened his eyes, and came to life again.

Elisha said to Gehazi, "Call the child's mother." So Gehazi did.

"Here is your son," Elisha said to the woman.

Oh, how thankful that mother was! And how happy she was as she carried her son downstairs.

What did a rich woman and her husband do for Elisha?
What did Elisha promise that God would give the woman?
What happened in the field one day that made the woman sad?
How did Elisha help the child?

STORY 55

# A Little Girl Helps Naaman

## 2 KINGS 5:1-17

The people in the land of Aram were enemies of the people of Israel. Naaman was an army leader in Aram. The king of Aram liked his army leader because he had won many battles. But Naaman had leprosy. He had sores on his skin that would not go away.

Sometime earlier, when the people of Aram won over Israel, they brought back with them an Israelite girl. She became a maid for Naaman's wife.

*Naaman rode in his chariot all the way to Elisha's house.*

One day the girl said to the woman, "I wish Naaman could go see God's prophet Elisha in Samaria, for he would take away Naaman's leprosy."

When Naaman heard what the little girl said, he told the king about it. So the king told him to go and see the prophet.

The army leader took silver and gold with him, and ten sets of new clothes. These gifts would be for the prophet if he could take away the leprosy.

Naaman rode in his chariot all the way to Elisha's house. But Elisha sent a messenger out to tell him, "Go and wash yourself seven times in the Jordan River. Then you will be healed of your leprosy."

The army leader was upset. "I thought Elisha would come out and put his hands on me. I thought he would pray that the Lord his God would make me well," he said. "Aren't the rivers in my own country better than all the rivers in the land of Israel?" He turned around and went away very angry.

But some of his men said to him, "Sir, if the prophet had told you to do some hard thing to make you well, wouldn't you have done it? But he has told you just to go and wash, and you will be healed. So why don't you at least try it?"

So Naaman went down to the Jordan River and dipped seven times. Suddenly his skin became new like a little child's, and the leprosy was gone! He went back to Elisha's house and said, "Now I know that there is no other God except the God of Israel."

Naaman wanted to give Elisha the gifts he had brought. Elisha said, "No, I won't take any gifts."

But Naaman wanted a gift from Elisha. He asked for two loads of dirt from the land of Israel to take home with him. He would make an altar from the dirt. And he would never again give an offering to any other god but the one true God, the Lord.

. . . . . . . . . . . . . . . . . . . . . . . . . . . . . . . . . . . . . . . . . . . . . . . . . . . . . . . . . . . . . . . .

**Who was Naaman, and why did he need help?**

**What good news did a little girl from Israel tell Naaman's wife?**

What did Elisha tell Naaman to do to be made well?

What happened to Naaman in the Jordan River?

Whom did Naaman say he would worship after that?

# Four Men Find Food for a City

### 2 KINGS 6:24-7:16; 17

It had been some time since Naaman from Aram visited Elisha in the Israelite city of Samaria. Now the king of Aram and his army came again to fight Samaria, as they often did. His soldiers were all around the city, so no one could get in or out. And there was no food in the city.

The Israelite king, Joram, was as wicked as his father, Ahab. That is why God sent terrible troubles to him and his people. Joram should have been sorry and asked God to help him. Instead, he blamed the troubles on Elisha.

King Joram came to Elisha's house. Elisha said that the next day there would be plenty of food, for the Lord had told him this.

That night four men with leprosy were sitting outside the city walls. They said to each other, "Why sit here with nothing to eat? If we go into the city, we'll die because there is no food. If we sit here, we will die. Come on, let's go out to the enemy army. If they don't kill us, we will be fine. If they do kill us it's okay, because we were going to die anyway."

So they went across the field to where the enemy army was camped. But no one was there! The Lord had made the soldiers from Aram hear the sound of another large army coming toward them. So they ran away in the night, leaving their tents and horses and everything else.

When the four men with leprosy found no one in the camp, they went into a tent and ate the food there. They took silver and gold and clothes and hid them. Then they went into another tent. They carried away more money and hid it, too. But then they stopped. "This isn't right," they said to each other. "We have good news, but we aren't telling our people."

So they went back to the city that night. They shouted to the people watching the gates, "We have been to the enemy camp, and no one is there!"

The people at the gates hurried to tell the king. But he said, "It's a trick. The enemy soldiers are hiding outside the camp. When we go over, they will hurry back and take us."

One of the king's helpers said, "Let's ride over and see." So the king sent a few of his men to the enemy camp, but no one was there. They looked as far as the Jordan River. All along the road were clothes and tools thrown away by the soldiers as they ran. Then the men returned to Samaria and told the king what they saw.

When the people heard about it, everyone ran out to the enemy camp. The Israelites brought back huge bags of flour and grain. So now the Israelites had plenty of food because four men shared their good news.

But after that, many bad kings ruled over Israel, one after another. And the people of Israel worshiped idols, just as the people around them did. God was angry with his people, but he waited and waited for them to do what was right. He sent prophets to warn them again and again of the terrible things that would happen if they didn't stop doing wrong.

At last the king of Assyria took the Israelites to live in his country far away. The kingdom of Israel had lasted about two hundred years. Then it came to an end.

...................................................................................................

Why were four men with leprosy hungry?

What did the four men find at an enemy camp?

How did the men help all of their people in the city of Samaria?

What bad things did the people of Israel do before their kingdom came to an end?

...................................................................................................

*The men with leprosy found food, silver, gold, and clothes in the camp.*

*Joash was the ruler instead of his wicked grandmother.*

# A Little Boy Becomes a King

## 2 KINGS 11–12;
## 2 CHRONICLES 22–24

We learned that many bad kings ruled the northern kingdom of Israel, which came to an end. Now let's go back to the story of the southern kingdom of Judah. There were many bad kings in Judah, too. And there was a wicked woman named Athaliah. Her father was King Ahab. She wanted to be the queen of Judah after her husband and son died. But instead, her grandson, baby Joash, was to become king.

The baby's aunt Jehosheba and uncle Jehoiada, a priest, hid the baby at the Temple. They took care of him until he was seven years old. Then Jehoiada said it was time to put a crown on the prince and make him king of Judah. So the priest did that. And he gave little King Joash a copy of God's laws. Then Joash was the ruler instead of his wicked grandmother, Athaliah. Everyone clapped and shouted, "Long live the king!"

Afterward, the priest and King Joash and all the people said that they would obey the Lord. They all began worshiping God at the Temple again.

When Joash grew older, he wanted to fix up the Temple of the Lord. He told all the priests, "Go into the cities of Judah and collect money from the people to fix up the Temple. And see that you hurry." But the priests didn't hurry.

Finally King Joash sent for Jehoiada the priest and asked him, "Why aren't the priests collecting money and fixing up the Lord's Temple?" Then the king said to make a big wooden box with a hole in the top. He said to set it at the door of the Temple. A messenger went all through the land of Judah, telling the people to bring money to the Temple as an offering to the Lord. Everyone was happy to come and drop some money into the box. Whenever it was full, Jehoiada the priest and one of the king's helpers counted it and put it in bags. They gave it to the men who were in charge of the builders.

As long as Jehoiada lived, he helped King Joash know how to do what was right. But after the priest died, the wicked leaders of Judah told King Joash they didn't want to worship God anymore. The wicked leaders talked him into letting them do what was very wrong. Then Joash said it was all right to worship idols instead of God.

Who took care of Joash when he was a little boy?

How old was Joash when he became the king of Judah?

When he grew older, why did King Joash have the people put money in a box?

After Jehoiada died, what did Joash do that was wrong?

STORY 58

# King Ahaz Closes the Temple

## 2 KINGS 16; 2 CHRONICLES 28–29

When Ahaz became the king of Judah, he didn't obey God. He worshiped idols instead. So the Lord sent the king of Aram against him. The enemy army took many people away from Jerusalem to the city of Damascus.

Other enemy armies began to fight against Judah too. Then Judah's King Ahaz took some of the silver and gold from the Temple and some nice things from his own palace. He sent them to the king of Assyria and asked him to fight against the enemies of Judah. The king of Assyria did as King Ahaz asked him to. He took the city of Damascus from the people of Aram. But it did not help Ahaz, because he was wicked and the Lord was against him.

After this, Ahaz became even more wicked. He broke up the beautiful furniture at the Temple and closed the doors so that no one could worship there. Then he placed idols all over Jerusalem and in every city throughout the land. The Lord was angry with Ahaz and the people of Judah for being so wicked.

Ahaz was king for sixteen years. When he died, his son Hezekiah became king.

Hezekiah did what was right and obeyed the Lord. As soon as he became king, he opened the Temple again. He called the priests back and told them to put everything where it belonged. Then the people could come and worship God again.

*Wicked King Ahaz closed the Temple doors so that no one could worship there.*

After working hard for about two weeks, the priests told the king, "It's all finished! All the cleaning has been done, the altar is ready for use, and we have brought back the gold and silver bowls that Ahaz took away. Everything is ready."

King Hezekiah got up early the next morning and went up to the Temple with the leaders of Jerusalem. They took with them seven young bulls, seven rams, seven lambs, and seven goats as an offering. Hezekiah commanded the priests to put the animals on the altar. He said to give them to God as a sacrifice for the sins of the people of Judah. He also told the priests to sing praises to the Lord. He told other priests to play cymbals, harps, and trumpets. As the offering was placed on the altar, the music began and everyone worshiped God.

Afterward the people brought their own offerings. And the priests offered these gifts to God for the people's sins. King Hezekiah and all the people were glad that God had helped them get the Temple ready quickly so they could worship him.

..................................................................................................

**Who came to fight against King Ahaz and the people of Judah?**

**What wicked things did King Ahaz do?**

**What good things did King Hezekiah do?**

..................................................................................................

*Hezekiah grew proud of his riches and power.*

# The Savior Will Come!

### 2 KINGS 20; 2 CHRONICLES 32:24-33; ISAIAH 53; MICAH 1; 5-6

One day King Hezekiah became very sick from a large sore that wouldn't go away. The prophet Isaiah told him, "The Lord says to get ready to die."

Hezekiah turned toward the wall. He prayed, "Lord, remember how I have tried to please you in all I do." Then he cried.

So the Lord told Isaiah to go back to Hezekiah and tell him, "I have heard your prayer, and I have seen your tears. I will make you well again. Three days from now you will be well enough to go to the Temple. And I will add fifteen years to your life!" So Isaiah gave the Lord's message to the king.

The king wanted to know for sure that this was going to happen. So Isaiah prayed for a sign from God. He prayed for the shadow on the palace steps to move backward ten steps. God answered his prayer!

Then Isaiah said to the king's helpers, "Use some figs to make a healing cream, and put it on the big sore." They did, and soon King Hezekiah was well again!

The king became rich and well known. He had many cows, sheep, and goats because God helped him in everything he did.

But Hezekiah grew proud of his riches and power. He acted as if he had gotten these things by himself, without God's help.

The king of Babylon sent messengers with letters and a present for him. Hezekiah was proud to have them visit him because they worked for a great king.

Isaiah the prophet asked Hezekiah, "What did these men want? And where did they come from?"

"They came from Babylon," Hezekiah replied.

"What have they seen in your palace?" Isaiah asked.

And Hezekiah answered, "Everything!"

Then Isaiah gave him this message from the Lord: "After you die, all your nice things will be carried to Babylon. Nothing will be left."

Hezekiah answered, "Whatever God does is right. At least there will be peace while I'm alive."

King Hezekiah told the people to put away their idols and worship the Lord. But soon they began praying to idols again. God sent the prophet Micah to speak to them.

"This is all that God requires," Micah said. "He wants the people of Israel to do what is right, to be kind and fair to each other, and to be humble and obedient to the Lord."

The prophets Micah and Isaiah both talked about the Savior. Micah said that the Savior would be born in the city of Bethlehem. And Isaiah said the Savior would die so that we can be forgiven for our sins. Many other prophets also told about the Savior hundreds of years before he was born. Because they did this, everyone can know that Jesus, the Savior, is the Son of God and that he was sent by God.

..........................................................................................................

What did God do with a shadow to show he would heal King Hezekiah?

What did Isaiah say would happen because Hezekiah showed off his nice things?

What did the prophet Micah teach about the Savior?

What did the prophet Isaiah teach about the Savior?

..........................................................................................................

STORY 60

# *King Josiah and the Lost Book*

DEUTERONOMY 31:9-13; 2 KINGS 22:1–23:3;
2 CHRONICLES 34

Josiah was eight years old when he became king of Judah. While he was still a boy, he began to do what pleased the Lord. When he was a young man, he went all through the land of Judah. He tore down the altars of Baal wherever he found them and got rid of the idols. He also traveled through the land of Israel and did the same thing there. (But most of the people of Israel were no longer living there, for they had been taken to Assyria.)

When Josiah came back to Jerusalem, he told his men to start fixing up the Temple. There was a lot of work to do, so the people brought gifts of money to pay the workers.

One day when the high priest was counting the money the people brought, he found a very special book. He said to one of the king's helpers, "I've found the Book of the Law! It was here in the Temple!"

Hundreds of years before this, Moses had written down the laws God gave him. God commanded that these laws must be read out loud to all the people every seven years. But the wicked kings and people of Judah didn't want to hear God's laws, so the book was lost and forgotten. Now the high priest found it and gave it to King Josiah's helper, who read it to the king.

*King Josiah learned that he and the people had not been obeying God.*

When King Josiah heard God's laws, he learned that he and the people had not been obeying God. The king tore his clothes and cried. Then he asked several helpers to go to the Temple to learn more about the Book of the Law.

At the Temple, the king's helpers talked to the prophet Huldah. She told them these words from the Lord: "I will get rid of this city, for the people have worshiped idols, and I am angry with them. But King Josiah, you were sorry when you learned you had not obeyed me. I heard you cry, so nothing bad will happen to the city as long as you live."

The helpers took God's message back to King Josiah. Then the king called all the people to come to the Temple. There he read God's book to them. Josiah promised to obey God's commandments. The people promised to obey all these laws from God too.

How old was Josiah when he became the king of Judah?

What book was lost and then found?

After the king read God's laws, what did he and the people promise to do?

STORY 61

# Jeremiah Writes
# a Message from God

2 KINGS 24:1-6, 18-20; 25:1-2;
2 CHRONICLES 36:4-21;
JEREMIAH 15; 21; 27; 29; 36

Once again, the people of Judah stopped obeying God. King Nebuchadnezzar of Babylon came to fight them. Then the king took some beautiful things from the Temple back to Babylon.

While Jehoiakim was the king of Judah, the Lord told the prophet Jeremiah to write about more terrible things that were going to happen to God's people. When the people saw those things written down, perhaps they would be sorry and turn back to God so he could forgive them. Jeremiah spoke God's words to Baruch, who wrote the message on a scroll. Then Baruch read it to the people at the Temple, and to the king's helpers.

King Jehoiakim asked one of his helpers to get the scroll and read it to him. He was sitting beside a fire. And as soon as his helper read one part of God's message, the king cut up that part with his knife and threw it into the fire. He wasn't sorry about the bad things he and his people had done. Instead, he was angry with Jeremiah and Baruch for writing these messages. So he sent some men to find them and put them in jail. But the Lord hid them.

Because the king burned God's messages, the Lord told Jeremiah that Baruch must write them again. So Jeremiah had Baruch write the same words down, and a lot more besides.

The people hated Jeremiah for telling them about their sins. He said to the Lord, "I have not hurt them. But they all say bad things against me."

Then the Lord promised that when the enemies of Jerusalem arrived to take the city, they would not hurt Jeremiah.

Another new king ruled in Judah for only three months. Then King Nebuchadnezzar of Babylon came to fight him. Nebuchadnezzar took away more beautiful things from the Temple and from the palace. He also took the king and his family, the leaders of Judah, the builders, and all the soldiers. He made them go to the faraway land of Babylon.

After they had gone, Jeremiah wrote a letter to them, telling them that God said they should build houses and plant gardens there. God said they would have to stay in Babylon and serve the king there for seventy years. But when the seventy years came to an end and they asked God to forgive their sins, he would bring them back to their own land.

Nebuchadnezzar left some people in Judah and made Zedekiah their king. He had to promise to obey Nebuchadnezzar, who went back to Babylon. But Zedekiah didn't do what he promised. So Nebuchadnezzar came back with his whole army. He made forts around Jerusalem. Then the people couldn't go in or out of the city.

Inside Jerusalem, King Zedekiah asked Jeremiah to pray that God would help them save their city. But Jeremiah told the king that Nebuchadnezzar would take over the city and burn it. If the people would give in to Nebuchadnezzar, they would not be killed.

The Lord told Jeremiah to wear a wooden yoke on his shoulders.

The Lord told Jeremiah to act out this message by wearing a wooden yoke on his shoulders. A yoke stands for hard work. So when the people saw Jeremiah wearing it, they understood that God was going to make them work hard for King Nebuchadnezzar. They would be his slaves and would have to do whatever work the king and his people made them do.

What did King Jehoiakim do to the scroll with God's message on it?

What did Jeremiah have Baruch do after the king burned the scroll?

How long did God say the people of Judah would live in Babylon?

What did it mean when Jeremiah wore a wooden yoke?

STORY 62

# *Jerusalem Burns*

## 2 KINGS 25; JEREMIAH 37–39; 52

The Lord gave this message to Jeremiah again: "Jerusalem will be taken and burned." Then the Lord said, "This is how I will show my anger to the people for their sins."

Some of the leaders of Judah told King Zedekiah that Jeremiah must be killed for saying such things. They said he made the people feel sad and afraid.

The king told the leaders to do as they liked with Jeremiah. So they let him down by ropes into a deep well that had a lot of mud at the bottom.

But one of the king's helpers said to the king, "Jeremiah may die of hunger in that well."

So the king sent thirty men to take Jeremiah out of the well, but they didn't set him free. They kept him in the palace prison.

*The leaders of Judah let Jeremiah down by ropes into a deep well.*

*Nebuchadnezzar's army burned the Temple in Jerusalem.*

Then King Zedekiah sent for Jeremiah again. The king said, "I want to ask you a question. Don't hide the truth from me."

Jeremiah answered, "If I tell you the truth, will you promise not to have me killed?"

"Yes," the king replied, "I promise."

So Jeremiah told him what the Lord said: "If you will give in to the king of Babylon and work hard for him, you and your family will be safe and Jerusalem won't be burned."

But King Zedekiah wouldn't obey and give in. So Nebuchadnezzar's army came to fight against Jerusalem for two and a half years. By the end of that time the food was all gone.

One night Zedekiah tried to get away from the city with his army, but he was caught. The mean king of Babylon and his men made Zedekiah blind. Then they put chains on him and took him to Babylon, where they kept him in jail until he died.

Nebuchadnezzar's army burned the Temple and the palace and all the homes in Jerusalem. They broke down the walls around the city and took the people away. Only the poorest people were left to work in the fields.

So the kingdom of Judah came to an end because of the sins of the people, just like the kingdom of Israel years earlier. Judah had lasted about 340 years, ever since Rehoboam was made king over the tribes of Judah and Benjamin. Of twenty rulers, fifteen were wicked, and only five obeyed the Lord. But even when there were good kings, the people often worshiped idols. The Lord gave them time to be sorry and sent his prophets to warn them, but they still wouldn't obey him. So at last he sent the people of Judah far away to Babylon. And, of course, the ten tribes of Israel were already in Assyria.

........................................................................................

Where did the leaders of Judah put Jeremiah because of the message he gave them from God?

What did King Nebuchadnezzar and his army from Babylon do to the city of Jerusalem?

Why did the kingdom of Judah come to an end?

........................................................................................

# *Dead Bones Come to Life*

### EZEKIEL 37

Before Jerusalem was burned down, a Jewish priest named Ezekiel was taken away to Babylon. God showed Ezekiel many strange things through visions. It was like having dreams when he was awake!

One day the Lord showed Ezekiel this vision. Ezekiel seemed to be in a valley where the ground was covered with the old, dry bones of dead people. The Lord asked him, "Can these bones live again?"

Ezekiel said, "Lord, only you know the answer to that."

Then the Lord told Ezekiel to say to the bones, "Dry bones, listen to what God says. I am going to put muscles on you and cover you with skin. I will put breath into you, and you will come to life. Then you will know that I am the Lord!" As soon as Ezekiel said this, a strange rattling noise began as the bones came together to form their skeletons. Then muscles grew on them and skin covered them. Soon the bones had bodies again, but they were still dead.

Then the Lord told Ezekiel to say to the winds, "Come and blow on these dead bodies so that they will have breath and live again." When Ezekiel said this, the wind blew and the dead bodies began to breathe. They came to life and stood up like a great army!

Then the Lord explained to Ezekiel what this vision meant. God said that his people, the Israelites, were like bones that were dry and dead. They had lost all hope of being happy or seeing their own land again. But the Lord would raise them up out of their troubles as he had raised those dry bones to life. "I will put my Spirit into their hearts and bring them back to their own land again. Then my people will know that I am the Lord. They will see that I have done what I promised."

After this the Lord told Ezekiel to get two sticks. He said to name one for the kingdom of Israel and the other for the kingdom of Judah. He told Ezekiel to hold the two sticks close together, and they would grow into one stick in his hand.

*Ezekiel talked to the dry bones, and they came together to form skeletons.*

Then God said to Ezekiel, "People will ask what this means. Tell them that I will bring my people back to their own land. They will not be divided into the two nations of Israel and Judah anymore, for I will make them one nation again. They will not worship idols anymore either. I will put my Spirit into their hearts and make them holy. They will be my people, and I will be their God. They will live in the land where their parents lived, and their children and grandchildren will live there always. I will be kind to them and give them a good king who will rule over them forever."

Who was Ezekiel?

How did God speak to Ezekiel?

In a vision, what did God tell Ezekiel to say to the dry, dead bones?

What did the vision mean that God was going to do for his people?

STORY 64

# Three Men in a Fire

## DANIEL 1–3

King Nebuchadnezzar of Babylon started a school to train some of the Jewish boys his people had taken from Jerusalem. Daniel and his friends Shadrach, Meshach, and Abednego were in that school. God helped them all become wise, and he helped Daniel understand the meaning of dreams.

When Daniel told King Nebuchadnezzar what one of the king's dreams meant, Nebuchadnezzar said to Daniel, "Your God is the God of gods. He is the King of all other kings." Then the king put Daniel in charge of the wise men and made Daniel's three friends rulers too.

Then, Nebuchadnezzar made a huge statue of gold and sent for his leaders. When they came, one of the king's helpers said, "The king

*"Now there are four men walking around in the fire!"*

commands you to bow down and worship his gold statue when the band begins to play. Anyone who won't do it will be thrown into a furnace with hot flames."

As soon as the band began to play, most of the leaders bowed down to worship the gold statue. But Daniel's three friends would not do it. They knew it was wrong to worship a statue.

Some of the Babylonians asked the king, "Didn't you make a law that says anyone who won't worship your statue will be thrown into a hot furnace? Well, some of your Jewish leaders won't bow down to your gold statue. Their names are Shadrach, Meshach, and Abednego."

King Nebuchadnezzar was very angry. He ordered the three young men to be brought to him. "Is it true," he shouted, "that you will not bow down to my gold statue? I'll give you one more chance. When you hear the band begin to play, you must worship the statue, or you will be thrown into a hot furnace. And what god will be able to save you?"

The three young men said to the king, "We won't do it! If you throw us into the furnace, our God is able to save us, and he will. But even if he doesn't, we will not worship your gods, sir, or bow down to your gold statue."

Nebuchadnezzar was very upset. "Heat the furnace seven times hotter than ever before!" he told his men. Then he called for the strongest soldiers in his army to tie up Daniel's friends and throw them into the furnace. It was so hot that the flames killed the soldiers. But after Shadrach, Meshach, and Abednego had fallen down into the fire inside the furnace, they got up and walked around in the flames! Only the ropes they were tied with burned up.

The king looked inside the furnace and couldn't believe what he saw. "Didn't we throw three men into the fire, tied with ropes?" he asked. "Now there are four men walking around in the fire! And the fourth looks like a son of the gods."

King Nebuchadnezzar shouted, "Shadrach, Meshach, and Abednego, servants of the Most High God, come out!"

So they came out of the furnace. The fire hadn't hurt them a bit. They didn't even smell of smoke.

Then the king said, "Praise to the God of Shadrach, Meshach, and Abednego, who has sent his angel and saved these young men who trusted in him. I now make a law to get rid of all people who say anything bad about the God of Shadrach, Meshach, and Abednego. No other God can save people as the God of these three young men can!" Then the king made the young men even greater leaders than they had been before.

What did Daniel's three friends tell the king they would not do?

What happened to the three men inside the hot furnace?

After God saved the men, whom did Nebuchadnezzar worship?

Then what did the king do for Daniel's friends?

STORY 65

# Daniel in the Lions' Den

DANIEL 6; 9

When Darius the Mede took over the kingdom of Babylon, the kingdom was ruled by 120 princes. Daniel was one of three leaders in charge of all the princes. Because Daniel was the best leader, Darius was planning to make him ruler over everyone. The other leaders and princes were upset and tried to find something bad to tell the king about Daniel. But they couldn't find that he did anything wrong. Finally they said to each other, "The only thing we could say against Daniel is that he worships his God."

So the princes and their leaders went to the king. They said, "King Darius, may you live forever! We want you to make a new law. Tell people they must pray only to you for the next thirty days. Anyone who doesn't obey will be thrown into a den of lions. Write this law down and sign it. Then not even you can change it." So King Darius signed the law.

*God sent an angel to shut the lions'*
*mouths so they would not hurt Daniel.*

Daniel knew that the law had been signed. But he still went home, opened the windows of his room, and got down on his knees to pray. Daniel prayed and gave thanks to God three times every day just as he always had.

Some of the king's helpers heard Daniel praying to God. So they hurried back to the king. They said, "Didn't you make a law that any person praying to anyone other than you must be thrown into a den of lions?"

"Yes," the king said, "I did. It is a law that can never change."

Then they said, "Daniel isn't obeying you. He prays to his God three times a day!"

Now the king was angry with himself for signing that law. He tried to find a way to save Daniel. But that evening the king's helpers said, "Our king, you know that the law cannot be changed."

So at last King Darius had Daniel thrown into a den of lions. But first the king said to him, "You worship God every day. May he save you."

After Daniel was thrown into the den, a big stone was rolled across the opening so that no one could get Daniel out.

When the king went to his palace, he wouldn't eat. And he couldn't sleep that night. So he got up early the next morning and hurried to the lions' den. He was afraid as he called out: "Daniel, you who worship the living God, was your God able to save you from the lions?"

Daniel called back to the king, "My God sent his angel to shut the lions' mouths so they couldn't hurt me!" Daniel had trusted God and was not hurt at all.

King Darius was so happy that he ordered his helpers to take Daniel out of the lions' den at once. Then the king sent this message to people all over the world. "I now make a new law that all people in my kingdom must worship Daniel's God. He is the living God, and his kingdom will last forever. He is the God who can save people from danger, for he saved Daniel from the lions."

While Daniel was in Babylon, he prayed that the Jews might return to the city of Jerusalem and build it again. He asked God to forgive them for their sins.

Some time later, the angel Gabriel came from heaven. He told Daniel that God heard his prayer and would soon send the Jewish people back to their own land. The angel also said that God would send a special ruler many years after that. It would be almost five hundred years before this would happen. Gabriel was telling about the time when Jesus, the Savior, would be born!

........................................................................................

Did Daniel pray to the king or to God?

How did God help Daniel in the lions' den?

What did King Darius's new law say?

What did an angel tell Daniel would happen around five hundred years later?

........................................................................................

STORY 66

# *Many Jews Return to Judah*

### EZRA 1–3; ISAIAH 44:21–45:13

At last the seventy years of living far from home came to an end for the people of Judah. In the land of Babylon, which was now called Persia, Cyrus was the king. Cyrus said he wanted the Jews to go home to Jerusalem. Nearly two hundred years earlier, when God's people were still

living in their own land, God had told his prophet
Isaiah to write about Cyrus. Isaiah wrote that a king
named Cyrus would let the people of Judah return
home.

Now King Cyrus sent this message to everyone
in his kingdom: "The Lord has told me to build
his Temple in Jerusalem again. All of God's people
may go back to the city of Jerusalem in the land of
Judah. You may go and build the Temple of the Lord
again. And those who don't go home should help
those who do go by giving them silver and gold and
cows. Also give them food and clothes."

Then the people of Judah got ready for their
trip to Jerusalem. Those who didn't want to go with
them gave them gifts. King Cyrus gave them more
than five thousand gold and silver bowls that had
been taken from the Temple.

More than 42,000 people returned to Jerusalem
with their leader, Zerubbabel. They took with them
more than 7,000 servants. They also took 736 horses,
245 mules, 435 camels, and almost 7,000 donkeys.

When they came to Jerusalem, they found that
the Temple, along with the houses and the city walls,
had been broken down or burned.

The first thing the people did was to rebuild the
altar of the Lord. They built it where the Temple
used to be so that they could worship God. They
offered gifts to God on the altar every day. They
offered one lamb in the morning and another lamb
in the evening, just as God's people had done before
they were taken to Babylon.

Then they got ready to build the Temple again.
They hired workers from Lebanon, just as King
Solomon had done hundreds of years before. The

*The workers cut down cedar trees on the Lebanon mountains.*

workers cut down cedar trees on the Lebanon mountains. Then they floated them in the sea to the shore near Jerusalem.

When the first stones for the bottom part of the new Temple were laid, the priests were so happy that they played their trumpets and cymbals and sang songs of praise to the Lord. The other people shouted praises to God. But many of the older priests and other leaders remembered the Temple that had stood there before. They couldn't keep back their tears as they thought about what had happened to it. So the shouting and the crying were both heard far away.

What did Cyrus let the Jewish people do?

What did the Jewish people find when they came back to Jerusalem?

Why were some people happy and some people sad about the new Temple?

# Queen Esther Talks to the King

### ESTHER

Some years later, the king of Persia was a man named Xerxes. Some of the Jewish people still lived in Persia. They had stayed there instead of going back to their own land of Judah.

Mordecai, a Jewish man, was a helper at the palace. He had a young cousin named Esther. The king loved Esther and made her queen, but he didn't know she was Jewish.

Haman, a man at the palace, was in charge of all the leaders. He didn't like Mordecai because Mordecai wouldn't bow down to him. Since Mordecai was Jewish, Haman asked the king to make a law to have all Jewish people killed. He said they did not obey the king's laws, but that was not true.

Mordecai heard about the law. So he asked Queen Esther to beg the king to save the lives of the Jewish people. Esther knew she could be killed for going to see the king when he had not asked her to come. But if he held out his gold rod to her, she would be safe. To help her be brave, Mordecai wrote her a message that said, "Who knows? Perhaps God made you queen at this time just so you can help the Jewish people."

*Queen Esther went to the king, and he held out his gold rod to her.*

Queen Esther went and stood in front of the king as he sat on his throne. God was with her, for the king held out his gold rod to her. He said, "Queen Esther, I will give you whatever you wish, even if it is half of my kingdom."

Esther answered, "Please come to dinner, and bring Haman with you."

So the king and Haman went to dinner with Esther. At the table the king asked Esther again, "What is it you wish?"

Esther answered, "Please come with Haman to another dinner tomorrow. Then I will tell you what I want."

When Haman went home, he called for his friends and for his wife. He bragged about how the king had made him more important than anyone else, and how Queen Esther had asked him to come to dinner two times. Then he said, "But I can't really be happy as long as Mordecai won't bow down to me."

His wife and friends said, "Make a place to hang Mordecai. And ask the king to let you do it."

Haman was pleased with this idea. So he had the work done. Then he went to the palace to talk to the king.

That night King Xerxes couldn't sleep. He told a helper to bring him the book about things that had happened while he was king. As the book was read to him, he learned that Mordecai had once saved his life.

When the king's helpers told him that Haman wanted to see him, he said, "Yes, tell him to come in." The king said, "Haman, what is the greatest thing I can do to honor a man who has helped me?"

Haman thought that he was the one the king wanted to honor. So he said, "Let one of your most important leaders put your robe on the man and lead him through the city streets on your horse. Have the leader shout, 'See how the king is honoring this man!'"

"Good!" the king said to Haman. "Take these robes and get my horse. Then do for Mordecai all the things you have talked about."

Well, there was nothing Haman could do but obey the king. So he put the king's robes on Mordecai and led him on horseback through the city streets. Haman shouted, "See how the king is honoring this man!"

Afterward Haman hurried home, hoping no one would see him.

At Queen Esther's second dinner, she told the king about Haman's plan to kill Mordecai and all the rest of her people. So the king said to hang Haman instead of Mordecai. Then the king said that the Jewish people could fight anyone who tried to hurt them. So they did. That's how God saved Queen Esther and her people.

What did Mordecai ask Queen Esther to do?

What might have happened to Esther if the king didn't want to see her?

What did the king tell Queen Esther?

What did Haman have to do for Mordecai?

How did the king help all of the Jewish people?

# A Time to Remember

### EZRA 7–8; NEHEMIAH

A Jewish priest named Ezra was living in Persia. He knew that many Jews had gone back to Judah to build the Temple again. So now he led more Jewish people back to the city of Jerusalem so he could teach God's laws to the people there.

Nehemiah, another Jewish man, worked for the king in Persia. When Nehemiah learned that the wall around Jerusalem had been torn down, he felt sad. So the king let him go back home too. He got his people together, and they built up the wall.

One day after the Jewish people had built the wall around Jerusalem, they met together near one of the gates in the wall. They asked Ezra the priest to bring from the Temple the book of God's laws that Moses had written down. So Ezra brought out the Book of the Law and stood up high where all the people could see him. Then he opened the book and read from morning until noon. Everyone listened—the men, the women, and the children, too. And the Levites explained what Ezra read.

When the people heard God's laws and remembered how often they had disobeyed them, they began crying. But Nehemiah and Ezra and the Levites said to them, "Don't cry, for this is a day to be happy and worship God. Don't be sad, for the joy of the Lord makes you strong. Go and enjoy some good food and sweet drinks. Share your food with those who don't have any." So all the people went to have a big dinner and to share their food. They were happy because now they could understand God's words.

The next day they came to Ezra again so that he could read more of God's laws to them. This time he read that they were to have a special festival each year. They were to make little shelters from tree branches. This was to remind them that their families from long ago had lived in the wilderness. There hadn't been such a happy festival in Jerusalem for many years.

Then the people remembered again how often they had disobeyed God. So they met once more. This time they were sad and went without food as they told God about their sins.

Their leaders wrote down their promise to obey all of God's commands. Nehemiah and many other leaders signed the promise.

Now the people had a new Temple in Jerusalem, where they could worship God. And they had a new wall around the city to keep them safe.

But several years later the people once again forgot their promise to obey God's laws. Nehemiah prayed and kept doing what he could to please God.

This chapter completes the story of the Old Testament.

...................................................................................

**Why did Ezra go back to Jerusalem?**

**Why did Nehemiah go back?**

**Why did the people cry at first when they heard God's words?**

**What made the people happy again?**

...................................................................................

*After King Herod fixed up the Temple again, it was even more beautiful.*

The Bible tells us nothing more about the Jewish people until Jesus was born more than four hundred years later. History books tell us that King Herod fixed up the Temple again and made it even more beautiful. He did it to please the Jews. And he did it just a few years before Jesus was born.

In the New Testament we will see how God kept his promises about sending Jesus, the Savior.

NEW TESTAMENT

The angel said, "You are going to have a baby boy,
and you are to name him Jesus."

# Three Visits from an Angel

### MATTHEW 1; MARK 1:1-3; LUKE 1

It was time for the Savior to come to earth. Everyone needed him, for no one was pleasing God. No one was obeying him. Everyone was a sinner, just as Adam and Eve had been. When Adam and Eve sinned in the Garden of Eden, God promised them that a Savior would come someday to take away their sins.

The prophets, too, had often told God's people that this wonderful Savior was coming. But the prophets said that someone else would come first. This person would tell the people to get ready for the Savior by turning away from their sins. The New Testament begins with the story of this man's parents.

## An angel visits Zechariah

An old priest named Zechariah worked at the Temple, helping the people to worship God. He and his wife, Elizabeth, were careful to obey all of God's commands, but God had never given them a child.

One day at the hour of prayer it was Zechariah's turn to go into the Holy Place where the gold altar was. Suddenly he saw an angel standing beside the altar! Zechariah was very afraid.

But the angel said, "Don't be afraid, Zechariah. I have come to tell you that God will give you and Elizabeth a son. You are to name him John. He will be filled with God's Holy Spirit from the time he is born. He will tell the Israelites about the Savior who is coming, and he will help many people turn from their sins and obey God."

"How can I be sure this will happen?" Zechariah asked the angel.

"I am Gabriel," the angel replied. "I live in heaven and stand close to God, doing whatever he commands me. He sent me to tell you this good news. And because you didn't believe me, you will not be able to speak until all that I have told you comes true."

## An angel visits Mary

Zechariah's wife, Elizabeth, had a young cousin named Mary. Six months after the angel talked to Zechariah in the Temple, God sent his angel to Mary. She was afraid, for she had never seen an angel before. But Gabriel said, "Don't be afraid, Mary! God has decided to bless you. You are going to have a baby boy, and you are to name him Jesus."

Mary didn't understand how she could have a baby, for she wasn't married and had never slept with a man. But the angel explained that baby Jesus would have no human father, for he would be the Son of God. Mary still didn't understand. But she said, "I will do whatever God wants."

## An angel visits Joseph

Mary was engaged to marry Joseph, a carpenter. When Joseph heard that Mary was going to have a baby, he was sad. He thought some other man was the baby's father. He would have to tell Mary that he couldn't marry her. But while he was sleeping, an angel told him that God was the baby's father, and the baby's name would be Jesus. The angel said it was all right for Joseph to get married to Mary after all. So he did, and he took care of Mary while she waited for her baby to be born.

What did the angel tell Zechariah?

What happened to Zechariah when he didn't believe the angel?

What did Mary say when the angel told her she was going to have a baby?

What was the angel's message to Joseph?

# John the Baptist Is Born

### LUKE 1:39-80

After the angle told Mary she was going to have a baby, Mary went to visit her cousin Elizabeth. Even though Elizabeth was an older woman, she was going to have a baby too, just as the angel had told her husband, Zechariah. The baby inside her jumped for joy when Mary came because he knew the baby inside Mary was very special.

Mary stayed with Elizabeth for about three months. Then she went back to her home in Nazareth.

Soon after Mary left, God gave Zechariah and Elizabeth the son he had promised them. When the baby was eight days old, Zechariah and Elizabeth's family and friends came to set him apart as God's child and to decide on his name. The people wanted to call the baby Zechariah, because that was his father's name. But his mother said, "No, we will name him John."

"Oh, no," they said to her, "no one in your family has that name." Then they talked to Zechariah with motions, asking him what he wanted to name the

*Zechariah and Elizabeth had the son God promised them.*

161

baby. Because he had not believed the angel, he couldn't speak yet. So he wrote these words: "His name is John." All of the people in the house were surprised, for they didn't know about the angel at the Temple who had given the baby this name. Suddenly Zechariah could talk again!

Little John grew, and the Lord blessed him. When he was older, he lived out in the lonely wilderness away from other people. He stayed there until the time came for him to preach to God's people and tell them about Jesus. This child God had given to Zechariah and Elizabeth was John the Baptist, the one who came to prepare the way for Jesus, the Savior.

Whom did Mary go to visit?

What could Zechariah do after he wrote that the baby's name was John?

What job did God have for John the Baptist after he grew up?

STORY 71

# Jesus, God's Son, Is Born

LUKE 2:1-21

The Jewish people were under the rule of the Romans. So they had to do whatever the Roman emperor and his leaders told them to. The emperor now made a law that the name and address of every person must be written down. He told all of the people to go to the cities where their families had lived many, many years before. Then the Roman officers could write down their names. So Joseph and Mary went to Bethlehem. That's because Joseph was from the family of King David, who had lived in Bethlehem hundreds of years before.

When Mary and Joseph came to Bethlehem, there was no place for them to stay. So they went out to a stable. That's where donkeys and camels and other animals slept. While Mary and Joseph were there, Mary's baby boy was born. He was the baby that the angel Gabriel had

*While Mary and Joseph were in the stable, Mary's baby boy was born.*

told Mary and Joseph to name Jesus. Mary wrapped the baby in strips of cloth and laid him in a manger. That's where the animals ate their food. But baby Jesus was safe in the manger.

That night some shepherds were in the fields outside of town. They were watching their sheep, keeping them safe from wild animals. Suddenly an angel came, and the brightness of God was all around them. The shepherds were terribly scared.

But the angel said, "Don't be afraid, for I have good news for you. It's for everyone in the world! Your Savior was born tonight in Bethlehem! His name is Christ the Lord. This is how you will know him. You will find him in a manger, wrapped in strips of cloth."

*Some shepherds were watching their sheep in the fields.*

Then suddenly many more angels came. They were all praising God and saying, "Glory to God! Peace on earth between God and those who please him."

After the angels returned to heaven, the shepherds talked together. They said, "Let's hurry to Bethlehem and find the baby." So they ran into town. Soon they found Mary and Joseph. And the baby was in a manger just as the angel had said he would be! Afterward the shepherds returned to their sheep. As they went back, they praised God for what the angels had told them and for the baby they had seen. He was the Savior.

When the baby was eight days old, Mary and Joseph named him Jesus. That was the name that the angel Gabriel had told them to give him.

---

Why did Joseph and Mary go to Bethlehem?

Tell about something special that happened in Bethlehem.

What is a stable, and what is a manger?

How did some shepherds learn about baby Jesus?

---

STORY 72

# *Simeon and Anna See Jesus*

LUKE 2:22-38

Baby Jesus was probably about six or seven weeks old when Joseph and Mary took him from Bethlehem to the Temple at Jerusalem. They worshiped God at the Temple. And they set baby Jesus apart as God's child, for he was the Son of God.

A wonderful old man named Simeon was at the Temple that day. Simeon loved God very much. For years he had been waiting to see the Savior whom God had promised to send. The Holy Spirit had promised Simeon that he would not die before seeing the Savior. So the Holy Spirit told Simeon to go to the Temple on the day Jesus' parents took him there.

*Simeon prayed, "Lord, your promise has come true. I have seen the Savior."*

165

When Simeon saw Joseph and Mary with baby Jesus, Simeon took the baby in his arms. He said, "Now, Lord, your promise has come true. I have seen the Savior. Now I can die in peace."

Also at the Temple that day was a very old woman named Anna. She was a prophet, so God sometimes told her about things that were going to happen in the future. For many years she had lived at the Temple so that she could worship there at any time, day and night.

Anna came in and saw Simeon holding the baby Jesus in his arms as he talked to Mary and Joseph. Then Anna began thanking God for letting her see God's Son. And she talked about Jesus to all of the people who were waiting for God to come and help them.

Where in Jerusalem did Mary and Joseph take baby Jesus?

What had Simeon been waiting for many years to see?

Why did Anna thank God?

STORY 73

# *Wise Men Visit a Little King*

## MATTHEW 2

It was some time after Jesus had been born. Now several wise men who knew how to study the stars came to Jerusalem from a land in the east. "Where is the child who is king of the Jews?" they asked. "We have seen his star and have come to worship him."

When King Herod heard them asking about a new king, he began to worry. He was the king, and he didn't want anyone else to have his job! He called for some teachers who had spent their lives studying the Scriptures. Then he asked them if the Bible said where the new king would be born.

"Yes," they replied. "One of the prophets wrote that it would be in the city of Bethlehem."

*The wise men gave presents to the new little king.*

So Herod said to the wise men, "Go to Bethlehem and look for the child. When you find him, come back and tell me so that I can worship him too!"

So the wise men went to Bethlehem. On the way, they were very happy when the star they had seen before came to them again. It went ahead of them and stopped right over a house. They went in and saw the young child with Mary, his mother. They bowed low before him, worshiping him. Then they gave presents to the new little king—special gifts of gold and spices. Afterward they returned to their own country. But they didn't go through Jerusalem, because in a dream God warned them not to tell King Herod where Jesus was. God knew that the king didn't really want to worship little Jesus. Instead, Herod wanted to kill the child so Jesus would never be able to take the king's place.

Then an angel of the Lord talked to Joseph in a dream. He told Joseph to hurry to Egypt with Mary and little Jesus. So Joseph woke them up in the night, and they left for Egypt. That's where they stayed until King Herod died. At that time an angel came to Joseph in a dream again and told him, "Go back to the land of Israel. The people who tried to kill Jesus are dead."

Joseph did as the angel said.

- - - - - - - - - - - - - - - - - - - - - - - - - - - - - - - - - - - - - - - - - - - -

Why did wise men come to Jerusalem from far away?

What was King Herod afraid that Jesus would do someday?

What did the wise men do when they saw Jesus in Bethlehem?

Where did an angel tell Joseph to take Mary and little Jesus?

- - - - - - - - - - - - - - - - - - - - - - - - - - - - - - - - - - - - - - - - - - - -

# Jesus Grows Up

## LUKE 2:39-52

When Joseph and Mary and the boy Jesus came back to Israel, they went to a town called Nazareth. That's where they lived while Jesus grew up.

Every year Joseph and Mary went to Jerusalem for the Passover festival. When Jesus was twelve years old, he went with them. Many other families also went to Jerusalem. They all went to celebrate and remember when God passed over the homes of the Israelites in Egypt, keeping their families safe.

After the special time came to an end, the people started walking back to their homes. Joseph and Mary saw that Jesus wasn't with them, but they thought he was with some of their friends, so they didn't worry. When evening came, they began asking if anyone had seen him. But no one had. By this time they were getting very worried.

They went back to Jerusalem to look for Jesus there. It took them a day to go back, and it was another day before they finally found him. He was at the Temple, talking with the great teachers there. He was listening to them and asking them questions. These men were surprised

*Jesus was at the Temple, talking with the great teachers there.*

at how much Jesus knew. After all, he was only twelve years old, and they had been teaching for many years.

Mary called to Jesus, "Son! Why have you treated us like this? We have been looking for you everywhere."

Jesus was surprised. He asked, "Didn't you know I would be here at my Father's house, the Temple?"

Joseph and Mary didn't understand what he meant. But when Jesus grew older, his mother remembered what he had said and often thought about it. Later, she understood it. Jesus was God's Son, so of course he would call the Temple his Father's house. And of course he would want to be there.

But for now, Jesus went back home to Nazareth with Mary and Joseph. He did all that they told him to do. And as he grew up, he grew tall and wise. God loved him, and people loved him too!

- - - - - - - - - - - - - - - - - - - - - - - - - - - - - - - - - - - - - - - - - - - - - - - -

**How old was Jesus when he first went to Jerusalem for the Passover?**

**What was Jesus doing when Mary and Joseph couldn't find him?**

**Why did Jesus call the Temple his Father's house?**

**As Jesus grew up, what are two ways he grew?**

- - - - - - - - - - - - - - - - - - - - - - - - - - - - - - - - - - - - - - - - - - - - - - - -

STORY 75

# *Jesus Is Baptized*

MATTHEW 3; MARK 1:4-15

The next we are told about Jesus, he was a man thirty years old. But only a few people knew that he was the Son of God, for John the Baptist hadn't started telling people about him.

At that time John was living alone out in the wilderness. His clothes were made of hair from camels. Around his waist he wore a leather belt.

*Something that looked like a dove came down from heaven.*

He ate big grasshoppers called locusts. And he ate honey made by wild bees.

But now the time had come for John to preach to the people. He would tell them to get ready for the Savior by turning away from their sins. He began preaching beside the Jordan River, where great crowds came to hear him. He told them that the Savior would soon be coming. The people must not think that their sins would be forgiven just because they came from a good family like Abraham's! No, they were to obey God.

Many who heard John preach were sorry for their sins and turned away from them. And John baptized the people in the river.

Then Jesus came to John and asked to be baptized, but John didn't want to do it. He said, "I need to be baptized by you. Why do you come to me?" He knew that Jesus had no sins to be washed away. So why should he be baptized?

Jesus told John to baptize him anyway. "We must do everything that is right," Jesus said. So John agreed.

When John baptized Jesus, the sky above Jesus opened. Something that looked like a dove came down from heaven and sat on him. It was the Holy Spirit. At the same time God's voice spoke from heaven, saying, "This is my Son. I love him very much, and I am very pleased with him."

Where did John live before he began preaching?

What did John tell the people they must turn away from?

Why didn't John want to baptize Jesus at first?

When John baptized Jesus, what did God send down from heaven?

What did God say about Jesus?

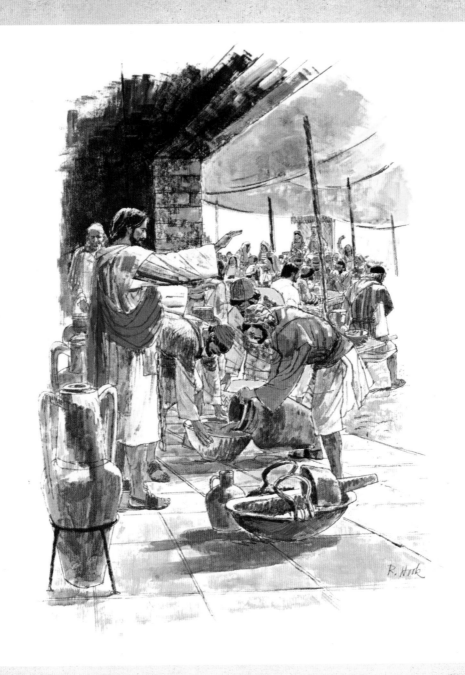

*Jesus told the servants, "Fill the jars with water,"
and the water became wine.*

# A Wedding

## JOHN 2:1-12

One day Jesus went to a wedding in the town of Cana. His mother and his followers went there too. During the wedding supper, the wine ran out. There was nothing more to drink. Jesus' mother told him about it. Then she told the servants to do whatever he told them to.

There were six large stone water jars at the house. People would use the water from jars like that to wash their hands before they ate.

Jesus told the servants, "Fill the jars with water." So they did. Then he said to take some to the person in charge of the wedding supper. When they did, the water had become wine!

The man in charge didn't know that Jesus had changed the water to wine, even though the servants did. So when he tasted how good it was, he called the bridegroom over. "I've never known of anyone who saved the best wine till the end!" he said. "Everyone else serves the best first. And after everyone has had enough, they serve the wine that isn't so good."

This was Jesus' first miracle. When his followers saw what he had done, they believed in him. They knew that no one but the Son of God could have done it.

Why did Jesus go to Cana?

Who went with Jesus to the wedding?

What did Jesus do at the wedding that no one but the Son of God could have done?

# A Night Visit

### JOHN 3:1-21

It was time for Jesus to go to Jerusalem for the Passover festival. The Jewish people celebrated this holiday every year.

Nicodemus was one of the leaders of the Jews. After dark one night, he came to see Jesus and said, "Teacher, we know God has sent you. You can do miracles, which show us that God is with you."

Jesus said, "Unless you are born again, you will never see God's Kingdom!"

"What?" Nicodemus asked in surprise. "How can a person be born a second time? Can he go back inside his mother's body as a tiny baby and be born again?"

Then Jesus talked about what he meant by being born again. He said that our parents give us life on this earth. But the Spirit of God gives us a new life from heaven. It's a life that will last forever.

Jesus said that he would be lifted up on a cross to die for our sins. He told Nicodemus how much God loves the people of the world: God sent his only Son into the world to die for everyone. God did it so that people who look up to Jesus and believe will not be punished for their sins. Instead, they will be forgiven and live forever in heaven after they die.

.......................................................................................................

**Who was Nicodemus?**

**What did Jesus say that surprised Nicodemus?**

**Who can give us new life so that it's like we are born again?**

**Why did God send his only Son, Jesus, into the world?**

.......................................................................................................

*Nicodemus came to see Jesus one night after dark.*

*The woman was surprised when Jesus told her*
*some of the things she had done.*

# Jesus Helps a Woman

### JOHN 4:1-42

One day Jesus and his followers came to a town in Samaria. Just outside the town was a well where people would go to get water. It was hot, and Jesus was tired. So he sat down by the well while his disciples went into town to buy food.

A woman carrying an empty jar came from the town to get some water. This woman had done many things that did not please God. Jesus knew this, because he knows everything about us. He told the woman some of the things she had done that did not please God. She didn't know yet that Jesus was God's Son, the Savior. So she was surprised. She said, "Sir, I see you are a prophet." She knew that Jesus must be a person to whom God told things that other people didn't know.

"I know that the Savior is coming into the world," the woman said to Jesus. "And when he comes, he will tell us everything."

Then Jesus told her, "I am the Savior!"

The woman left her water jar and hurried back to town. She said to the people, "Come and see a man who told me everything I ever did! Could this be the Savior?"

The people hurried out to the well to see Jesus. When they heard him, they asked him to please stay for a while. So he stayed in the town for two days, and the people listened carefully to what he taught them. Then they said to the woman, "We, too, believe Jesus is the Savior. But it's not just because of what you told us about him. We have heard him for ourselves, and now we know that he is the Savior from heaven."

What did Jesus tell the woman at the well about herself?

What did he tell the woman about himself?

What did the woman at the well tell the people in town about Jesus?

Why did the people from town believe Jesus is the Savior?

# Jesus Helps a Father

## JOHN 4:43-54

Jesus returned to the town of Cana, where he had changed water into wine. A rich man heard that Jesus had come. The rich man was from the city of Capernaum, more than ten miles away. But the man traveled all the way to Cana because he had something important to ask Jesus. He wanted Jesus to make his son well. His son was very sick. "Please come quickly before my child dies," the rich man said.

But Jesus told the man, "Go home, because your son is already well again. He will not die. He will live!"

The man believed Jesus, so he started back home. But before he got there, his servants met him. They said, "Your son is well!" He asked them what time the child had started to get better. They answered, "Yesterday at about one o'clock in the afternoon the fever left him."

The man knew that this was the same time Jesus had said to him, "Your son will live!" So the rich man and all his family believed in Jesus as the Son of God.

What did a rich man want Jesus to do?

What did Jesus tell the man?

What time was it when Jesus said the man's son would be well?

When did the rich man's son get well?

*Jesus told the man, "Go home, because your son is already well again."*

*All those fish were too heavy for the nets.*

# Finding Fish

### MATTHEW 4:18-22; MARK 1:16-20; LUKE 5:1-11

When Jesus came to the Sea of Galilee near the town of Capernaum, big crowds of people came to hear him preach. There were so many people that they almost pushed Jesus into the water. Then he noticed two fishing boats along the shore. Near the boats were the fishermen, washing their nets. So Jesus stepped into one of the boats—it belonged to Peter. He asked Peter to push his boat out a little way into the water. Then Jesus sat down and taught the people from the boat.

When he had finished, he told Peter and his brother, Andrew, to go out on the lake. Jesus said to let down their nets and they would catch many fish.

Peter answered, "Sir, we fished all night and didn't catch a thing. But if you say so, we'll try again." They were surprised that in just a little while they had caught many fish. All those fish were too heavy for the nets, and the nets began to tear. Peter and Andrew shouted to their partners, James and John, who were in the other boat. They asked their friends to come and help them. They all worked together, filling both boats with fish until they almost sank from the weight of all those fish!

When Peter saw the miracle Jesus had done, he got down on his knees and worshiped Jesus.

Where did Jesus sit and teach a large group of people?

What did Peter say when Jesus told him and Andrew they would catch many fish?

Why did Peter and Andrew need help from their two partners?

Why did Peter worship Jesus?

*Jesus said to the fishermen, "Come with me.*
*I'll show you how to find people instead of fish."*

# Finding People and Working Hard

### MATTHEW 12:9-15; MARK 1:16–2:12; 3:1-19; LUKE 5:1-11, 17-26; 6:6-13

Jesus had helped Peter and Andrew find a lot of fish. Now Jesus said to the fishermen, "Come with me. I'll show you how to find people instead of fish." Jesus asked James and his brother, John, to follow him too. So all four fishermen left their boats, their nets, and everything else. They went with Jesus and followed him everywhere because they were Jesus' disciples now.

One day Jesus went to the home of Andrew and Peter. James and John were there too. Peter's mother-in-law was sick in bed with a high fever. The men wanted Jesus to help her. So he went and stood beside her bed. He took her by the hand and helped her to sit up. Right away she became well, and she got up and cooked dinner for everyone!

After sunset, a big crowd of people gathered in front of the house. They brought many sick people to Jesus so he could make them well. They brought people with evil spirits, too. The crowd watched as Jesus made sick people well and sent evil spirits away.

In the morning, long before it was light, Jesus went out to a lonely place to pray. Even though he was God's Son, he was living on the earth as a man. And he needed to pray for God's help just as the rest of us do.

While he was away, many people looked for Jesus. When they found him, they asked him not to leave. But Jesus said, "I must go and preach the Good News about God's Kingdom in other places too."

So Jesus traveled to different cities, where he preached to large crowds and made sick people well. When he came back to the city of Capernaum, Jesus healed a man who couldn't walk. And on the Sabbath day of worship, he healed a man who had a small hand that he couldn't use.

The Jewish leaders became angry. They were upset because Jesus had healed a man on the Sabbath, the day that God had told his people to rest. They didn't pay any attention to Jesus when he said, "If one of your sheep fell into a well on the Sabbath, wouldn't you pull it out? A person is much more important than a sheep! So of course it is right to do good on the Sabbath."

The angry leaders began to talk about killing Jesus. So he and his disciples went away to the Sea of Galilee. Many people from many places came to see Jesus when they heard of the wonderful things he did. The sick people crowded around him to touch him, because when they did, they got well!

One night Jesus went up on a mountain by himself. He stayed there until morning, praying to God. Then he called his disciples to him. He chose twelve of them to be special friends and helpers who would be with him all the time. He would teach them to preach and do miracles. The twelve were called "apostles," and these were their names:

Peter
Andrew (Peter's brother)
James (son of Zebedee)
John (James's brother)
Philip
Bartholomew
Thomas
Matthew (the tax collector)
James (son of Alphaeus)
Thaddaeus
Simon
Judas Iscariot

What did Jesus ask the four fishermen to do?

How did Jesus help Peter's mother-in-law?

What did Jesus do all night before he chose his twelve special helpers?

What were the twelve special disciples called? How many of them can you name?

# Jesus Teaches from a Hill

## MATTHEW 5–7; LUKE 6:20-49

When Jesus saw crowds of people coming to him, he climbed a hill. He began teaching his disciples by saying:

God blesses those who realize their need for him, for the Kingdom of Heaven is given to them.

God blesses those who are gentle, for the whole earth will belong to them.

God blesses those who are merciful, who care for others, for they will be shown mercy. God will be kind to them.

God blesses those whose hearts are pure, for they will see God.

God blesses those who work for peace, for they will be called God's children.

Jesus also taught his followers how to pray. His words are called the Lord's Prayer:

Our Father in heaven, may your name be honored.

May your Kingdom come soon.

May your will be done here on earth, just as it is in heaven.

Give us our food for today.

And forgive us our sins, just as we have forgiven those who have sinned against us.

And don't let us give in to temptation, but save us from the evil one.

*[Parents, you may want to repeat the Lord's Prayer using the words you say in your church.]*

Jesus continued teaching the people. He said that when others are unkind to us and hurt us, we must not hurt them back. Instead we must do good things for them and pray for them and love them. Then we will be acting like true children of our Father in heaven.

Jesus told his disciples not just to pretend to be nice in order to get praise for it. Instead, we should please God by really being nice to others.

Then Jesus said we must send our money ahead of us to heaven. How do we do this? By giving money to our church and Sunday school and to missionaries and to poor people. If we do these things, someday in heaven we will have more things to make us happy than all the money in the world can buy.

Jesus talked again about how to treat other people. He said it is very important to treat others the way you would like them to treat you.

Jesus also told an important story about two men. Each of them built a house. The wise man built his house on a rock. When he had finished it, a big storm came up. But the rain and wind could not hurt the house because it was built on a solid rock.

The foolish man built his house on sand. When the storm came, the rain washed away the sand beneath his house, and the wind blew against the house. So it fell down with a big crash.

Jesus said that if we listen to his teaching and do what he tells us to do, we are like the wise man who built his house on the rock. But those who listen to Jesus without obeying him are like the foolish man who built his house on the sand. Those who do what Jesus says will be saved. They will live safely in heaven someday. But those who don't obey him will not have a home in heaven.

...................................................................................................................

**What kinds of people does God bless?**

**What are some things Jesus teaches us to pray about?**

**How does Jesus want us to treat people who are unkind?**

**How can we be like the wise man who built his house on a rock?**

...................................................................................................................

*After Jesus climbed the hill, he began teaching his disciples.*

# A Farmer's Seeds and God's Words

## MATTHEW 13:1-23; MARK 4:1-20; LUKE 8:1-15

Jesus often told stories with lessons about God. These stories are called parables.

One day big crowds of people followed Jesus as he walked along the shore of the lake. So he got into a boat and taught the people from there. He told them this story.

A farmer went out into the field to plant some seeds. Some of the seeds fell on a path where the dirt was hard. Then birds flew down and ate the seeds.

Some of the seeds fell around stones and rocks. The seeds began to grow into little plants. But there wasn't enough dirt on top of the rocks for strong roots to grow down into the earth. So the little plants dried up and died.

And some of the seeds fell where weeds were growing. The seeds began to grow, but the weeds shut out the sunshine the plants needed. So these little plants soon died too.

But some of the seeds fell on good ground. There was plenty of soft dirt that was ready for the seeds. The rain watered those seeds and the sun warmed them. Soon they grew bigger and bigger. And after a few months there was a large crop of grain. There was a hundred times as much as the farmer had planted!

When Jesus was alone with his disciples, they asked him to explain this parable to them. He told them that the seeds are like God's words. And the farmer is the one who brings God's words to people.

Some of the people who hear God's words have hard hearts like the hard path. They won't believe God's message. Just as the birds ate the seeds that fell on the hard path, these people let Satan take God's words away. He makes them think that other things are more important than God.

Others who hear God's words are happy to hear them at first, and they try to obey him. But as soon as they have trouble or hear others laughing at them, they turn away from God. They are like the places with stones and rocks.

Some people hear God's words and are glad. But afterward they begin to care more about their money and their things than they do about God. These things crowd Jesus out of their lives, just as weeds can crowd out many seeds.

But some people listen carefully to everything God says. They remember his words and try every day to please him by obeying him. They are like good soil, where seeds grow well and there is a crop of up to one hundred times as much seed as the farmer planted.

*A farmer went into the field and planted some seeds.*

Can you name the four kinds of places where seed fell in Jesus' story?

What did Jesus say the seeds in his story were like?

When you hear God's words, which kind of ground do you want to be like?

189

*Jesus stood up and spoke to the wind and the water.*

# A Storm on a Lake

MATTHEW 8:23-27; MARK 4:35-41;
LUKE 8:22-25

It was evening when Jesus and his disciples got into a boat. They began sailing over to the other side of the Sea of Galilee. But suddenly the wind began to blow very hard, and there was a terrible storm on the lake. High waves came up over the sides of the boat. Soon it was getting full of water and beginning to sink. But Jesus was asleep at the back of the boat.

"Teacher!" the disciples shouted at him. "Save us! We'll all be drowned!"

Then Jesus stood up and spoke to the wind and the water. He said, "Be quiet!"

The wind stopped blowing, and the water became very still and quiet. There were no more high waves, so water wasn't coming into the boat anymore. Then Jesus asked his disciples, "Why were you afraid? Why do you have so little faith?"

Even though the disciples were Jesus' friends, it was hard for them to understand how Jesus could make the wind and the water obey him. They still didn't know that Jesus was God's Son, and that he could do anything! They asked each other, "Who is Jesus anyway? How did he do that?"

**What was Jesus doing when the storm began?**

**How did Jesus stop the storm?**

**Why didn't Jesus' disciples need to be afraid?**

# A Woman and a Girl Meet Jesus

### MATTHEW 9:18-26; MARK 5:21-43; LUKE 8:40-56

When Jesus came back to Capernaum, one of the leaders of the synagogue—the Jewish place of worship—came to Jesus. The man got down on his knees and said, "My little girl is very sick, and I'm afraid she is going to die. Please come and put your healing hands on her so that she will get well."

Jesus and his disciples went with the father. A big crowd of people followed along.

In the crowd was a woman who had been sick for twelve years. She had given doctors all her money, but she was getting worse instead of better. When the woman heard that Jesus was in town, she said to herself, *If I can only touch him, I'll get well.* So she pushed her way through the crowd. As soon as she touched Jesus, her sickness was gone.

Jesus felt the healing power go out of him, so he turned around and asked, "Who touched me?"

*Jesus said, "Get up, little girl!"*

The disciples said, "The whole crowd is pushing against you!" But Jesus kept looking around to see who had done it. The woman knew what had happened. She was shaking as she came to Jesus and told him what she had done.

"Daughter, don't be afraid," Jesus said to her. "Because of your faith in me, you are well."

He was still talking to the woman when messengers came to tell the father of the sick girl, "Your child has died. There is no need for Jesus to come now."

But Jesus told the father, "Don't be afraid. Just trust me."

When they came to the house, Jesus saw the people and heard them crying. He said to them, "Why cry? The child isn't dead. She is only asleep!" He meant that she would soon be alive again, like someone waking up from sleep. But the people didn't believe him, so they laughed at him.

Then Jesus told the people to go outside. He told three of his disciples—Peter, James, and John—and the girl's father and mother to come with him into the room where she lay. Jesus took the girl by the hand and said, "Get up, little girl!" And the girl, who was twelve years old, jumped up and started walking! Her parents were so happy they didn't know what to do. So Jesus told them, "Give her something to eat."

................................................................................

**What did the father of a sick girl want Jesus to do?**

**On the way to the girl's house, how did Jesus help a woman in the crowd?**

**After the girl died, what did Jesus do to help her?**

................................................................................

# Dinner for a Crowd

MATTHEW 10; 14:13-21; MARK 6:6-13, 30-44;
LUKE 9:1-6, 10-17; JOHN 6:1-16

Jesus sent his twelve disciples all through the land to preach the Good News. They went out to the cities and towns, preaching to the people and making sick people well. When they came back, they told Jesus about everything they had done.

"Let's get away to some quiet place where you can rest for a while," Jesus said. There were so many people coming and going that Jesus and his twelve special helpers didn't even have time to eat.

So they all got into a boat and sailed to the other side of the Sea of Galilee, where they could be alone. But many people saw where Jesus was going, so they walked around the lake and met him there.

Jesus could see that the people needed him, just like sheep need a shepherd. So he told them about God, his Father. He kept on teaching until late in the day.

Then his disciples came to him. They said, "Send the people away so they can buy food, for it will soon be dark."

"They don't need to go away," Jesus said. "You feed them! Philip, where can we buy bread for everyone?" Jesus already knew what he was going to do, but he wanted to hear what Philip would say.

Philip said, "It would take a lot more money than we have to feed all this crowd!"

Then Peter's brother, Andrew, said that a young boy in the crowd had five loaves of bread and two small fish. But he knew that wouldn't feed many people.

Jesus told the disciples to have the people sit down in groups on the green grass. Then Jesus took the five loaves and two fish, looked up to heaven, and thanked God for the food. He broke the loaves into pieces and gave some bread and fish to the disciples. Then they passed the food around to the people. And the strangest thing happened. As the disciples

*The disciples passed the food around to the people,*
*and everyone had plenty to eat.*

broke off pieces of bread, the loaves were still the same size as before, so there was enough for everyone! And it was the same with the fish.

About five thousand men had dinner that day. The women and children with them had dinner too. And the food all came from the five loaves and two fish. Everyone had plenty to eat, and there were even twelve baskets of bread left over!

What food was in the boy's lunch?

How many people did Jesus feed with the boy's lunch?

Why could Jesus feed so many people with such a little lunch? (Hint: Who is Jesus' Father?)

STORY 87

# The Good Samaritan

### LUKE 10:25-37

One time when Jesus was teaching people, a man who knew God's law very well came to him. The man asked this question to test Jesus: "Teacher, what must I do to live forever?"

"What does God's law say?" Jesus asked him.

The man said, "You must love God with all your heart and all your soul. You must love him with all your strength and all your mind. And you must love your neighbor as much as you love yourself."

"Right!" Jesus replied. "Do that and you will live."

"But who is my neighbor?" the man asked.

Jesus answered by telling him this story:

A Jewish man was traveling from Jerusalem to Jericho, but some robbers stopped him. They took his clothes and money and beat him up. They left him half-dead beside the road.

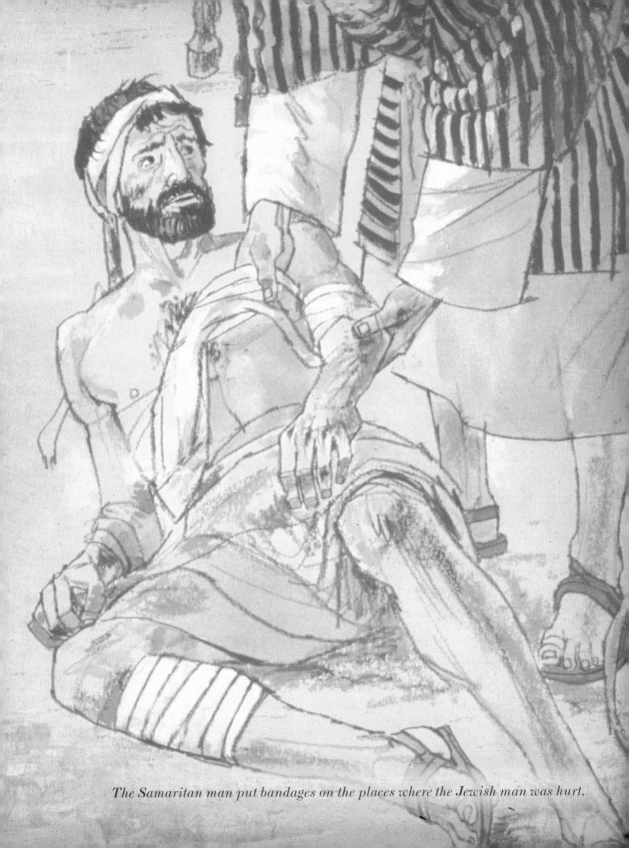

*The Samaritan man put bandages on the places where the Jewish man was hurt.*

While he lay there on the ground, too weak to get up, a Jewish priest went by. He was a teacher of God's law. But instead of being kind to the hurt man, he crossed over to the other side of the road. He went on his way, as if he didn't see the man. Next, a worship leader from the Temple came along. This Levite saw the hurt man beside the road. But he, too, went to the other side. He kept right on walking without trying to help.

But then a Samaritan man came by. The Jews and Samaritans didn't like each other. But when the Samaritan saw the hurt Jewish man, he felt sorry for him. The Samaritan put medicine and bandages on the places where the man had been hurt. Then he put the man on his donkey. He took the man to an inn, where he stayed that night, taking care of the hurt man. The next day he paid the man's bill. And he asked the person in charge of the inn to care for the hurt man until he was well again. The Samaritan said he would pay the rest of the bill the next time he came to the inn.

At the end of his story, Jesus asked, "Which of the three men was a neighbor to the hurt man?"

"The one who helped him," said the man who knew all about God's law.

Then Jesus told him, "Go and do the same for everyone who needs your help."

......................................................................................

**Why was it a surprise that a Samaritan man would help a Jewish man?**

**What did the Good Samaritan do for the Jewish man who had been hurt?**

**What does Jesus want us to do for the people all around us?**

......................................................................................

# Mary Listens to Jesus

### LUKE 10:38-42

Jesus and his disciples came to the town of Bethany, which was near Jerusalem. Jesus always liked to stop there to visit two sisters named Martha and Mary. They also had a brother named Lazarus.

When Jesus came, Mary sat by his feet and listened to him. She wanted to hear him tell about God and his Kingdom.

But Martha was worried about the big dinner she was getting ready. She was angry with her sister for not helping. She said to Jesus, "Lord, don't you care that Mary has left all the work for me to do? Tell her to come and help me."

But Jesus said, "Martha, Martha, you get upset so easily. Only one thing is important. Mary has chosen it, and I won't tell her to stop. I will let her keep listening to me."

*Mary sat and listened to Jesus, but Martha was angry with her sister for not helping.*

Where did Mary and Martha live?

Why was Martha angry with her sister?

What did Jesus want Mary to keep doing?

Jesus said, "If you lose one sheep, don't you leave all the others and hunt for the lost one?"

# Jesus, the Good Shepherd

## LUKE 15:3-7; JOHN 10:1-30

One day Jesus was talking to some people about sheep and how they listen to their shepherds. He said, "I am the good shepherd. I know my sheep, and they know me." He meant that he is like a shepherd to his disciples, and they follow him like a flock of sheep. Shepherds stay with their sheep night and day to keep them from getting lost and to keep them safe from wild animals. Just like a shepherd, Jesus keeps his followers safe. He keeps us safe from Satan and helps us find our way to heaven.

Jesus went to the Temple another time and talked to the Jewish leaders. They crowded around him and asked, "If you are the Son of God, why don't you say so?"

Jesus answered, "I have, but you won't believe me. That's because you are not my sheep. My sheep listen to my voice and follow me, and I give them life that lasts forever. They will never be lost. My Father gave them to me, and no one can ever take them away from me. My Father and I are one." Jesus meant that he is God. He is not God the Father, but God the Son. Jesus, God's Son, is as good and as great as God the Father.

On another day Jesus had this to say: "If you have one hundred sheep and lose one of them, don't you leave all the others and hunt for the one that is lost? And when you find it, you put it on your shoulders and joyfully carry it home! After you get home, you tell all your neighbors and friends, and they are happy with you, because you have found your lost sheep. Well, that's the way it is with people who sin by doing bad things. They are like lost sheep. There is joy in heaven when even just one sinner is sorry about doing bad things and stops doing them."

**What does a shepherd do for his sheep?**

**What does Jesus do for his followers?**

**What do we do that makes us like lost sheep?**

**What can we do to bring joy in heaven?**

# A Young Man Runs Away

LUKE 15:1-2, 11-32

In Jesus' time, the tax collectors cheated people whenever they could. One day some tax collectors came to hear Jesus, and the Jewish leaders were upset. They asked, "Why is Jesus kind to these men who do such bad things? He even eats with them!"

So Jesus told this story:

A man had two sons. The younger son said to him, "Father, give me my share of the money you are planning to give my brother and me." So his father did. Then this younger son went to a country far away. He did bad things and spent all of the money from his father.

There was no rain, and crops wouldn't grow where the young man was living. So he couldn't get enough food to eat. He began working for a farmer, feeding the pigs. He was so hungry he wanted to eat what the pigs ate. But no one gave him any food.

Finally he said to himself, "At home even the men who work for my father have plenty to eat. And here I am with no food. I'll go to my father and tell him that I have sinned against him and against God. I'll tell him I'm not good enough to be called his son anymore. But I'll ask him to let me work for him."

So the young man went back home. While he was still far away, his father saw him and ran out to meet him. Then his father hugged him, and he began his speech. "Father, I have sinned against God and you, and I don't deserve to be called your son anymore. . . ."

But his father said to the servants, "Bring out the best clothes in the house, and get some sandals. Then fix the best meat we have, and let's have a party. This son of mine was lost, but now he is found." So they had a big dinner.

*The father ran out to meet his son and hugged him.*

When the older son came home from working in the fields, he heard the music and dancing. So he called to one of the servants and asked what was going on.

"Your brother is back!" the servant told him. "And your father is having a big party for him."

The older son was angry and wouldn't go in. His father came out, and the older son said, "I've worked hard for you all my life, and I've always obeyed you. But you never once gave a party for me. Now this other son of yours comes back after doing all sorts of bad things, and you have a party for him."

The father said, "Son, I've always loved you. Everything I have is yours. But we should be happy today, because your brother has come home. It's as if he came back to life! He was lost, and now he has been found."

Jesus told this story because he wanted the Jewish leaders to know that God loves sinners and will forgive them. God will let them be his children if they will stop doing bad things, come back and talk to him, and start obeying him.

In Jesus' story, what did the younger son do with the money from his father?

When the son came home, how did his father welcome him?

What did the father say to the older son, who was angry?

When we've done bad things, will God still love us?

# *Jesus and Lazarus*

### JOHN 10:39–11:45

Jesus left Jerusalem for a while. He was preaching to people on the other side of the Jordan River. Many of the people there believed in him.

About that time, Lazarus, who was Mary and Martha's brother, became very sick. His sisters sent a message to Jesus to tell him about it. Jesus loved Lazarus and Lazarus's sisters. But when he heard how sick Lazarus was, he stayed where he was for two more days. He waited so that when he went back, people would see God's power working through him.

Then he said to his disciples, "Now let's go to Bethany. Our friend Lazarus is sleeping, and I am going to wake him up." Jesus meant that Lazarus had died and that he was going to bring Lazarus back to life again. But his disciples thought he meant Lazarus was resting.

Then Jesus told them plainly, "Lazarus died."

Many people had gone to Bethany to be with Martha and Mary, who were very sad. When Martha heard that Jesus had finally come, she went out to meet him. "Lord, if you had been here, my brother wouldn't have died. But I know that even now God will give you whatever you ask."

Jesus told Martha, "Your brother will live again."

"Yes, of course," Martha said. "He will live again when everyone else does—at the end of time."

Then Jesus said that he is the one who brings life. "People who believe in me will live again. They will live forever after they die. Do you believe this?"

Martha said, "Yes, Lord. I believe in you. I believe that you are God's Son and that he sent you into the world."

Then Martha went back to the house. She told Mary that Jesus had come and wanted to see her. So Mary ran out to Jesus and got down on her knees at his feet. "Lord, if you had been here, my brother wouldn't have died."

When Jesus saw Mary and the other people crying, he was upset. "Where have you buried Lazarus?" Jesus asked.

*Lazarus walked out of the cave where he had been buried.*

"Lord, come and see," the people said.

Then Jesus cried. Some people said, "See how he loved his friend." But others said, "This man helps blind people see. Couldn't he have saved Lazarus from dying?"

Lazarus's body was in a cave. A stone had been rolled across the opening.

"Roll the stone away," Jesus said.

Some of the men rolled the stone away. Jesus shouted, "Lazarus, come out!" And Lazarus came back to life! He walked out of the cave where he had been buried. His head and hands and feet were wrapped up in the cloths he had been buried in. "Take the cloths off," Jesus told the people, and they did.

When the people who were with Martha and Mary saw this great miracle, many of them finally believed in Jesus.

........................................................................

**After Lazarus died, what did both Martha and Mary say when they saw Jesus?**

**Tell how Jesus helped Lazarus.**

**After people who believe in Jesus die, what will happen to them?**

........................................................................

STORY 92

# *Jesus Heals Ten Lepers*

LUKE 17:11-19

Jesus and his disciples were walking along a road one day when ten men with leprosy came to meet Jesus. The lepers had sore spots all over their skin. They knew they were not supposed to get too close to other people. If they did, the other people might get sores too. So they stood a little way off and shouted, "Jesus, Master, please show us that you care about us. Please help us."

Jesus heard the men shouting to him. He called back to them, "Go and show yourselves to the priests." Jesus said this because if the lepers got well, they had to

*Only one of the men came back to thank Jesus for making him well.*

207

let a priest see them. If the priest said they were well, they could go back to their families.

As these ten men were going to see the priest, the sores on their skin went away! But only one of the men came back to thank Jesus for making him well. That man was a Samaritan.

Jesus asked, "Didn't I make ten men well? Where are the other nine?" Then Jesus told the man, "Stand up and go. You believed in me, and your faith has made you well."

Why couldn't the ten men with leprosy get close to other people?

How many lepers did Jesus make well?

How many of the men said thank you to Jesus?

STORY 93

# *Children Love Jesus*

### MATTHEW 19:13-15; MARK 10:13-16; LUKE 18:15-17

Sick people weren't the only ones who wanted to see Jesus. Some parents knew how special he was, so they brought their little children to him. They wanted Jesus to put his hands on them and bless them. But his disciples tried to send them away.

Jesus was upset with his disciples. "Let the little children come to me," he said. "Don't send them away, for the Kingdom of God belongs to everyone who is like these children." Jesus meant that the only way to get into God's Kingdom is to love him and trust him the way children do.

Then Jesus picked up the children. As he held each one in his arms, he placed his hands on the child's head and prayed for that child. He blessed all of the children who came to him.

*Jesus blessed each child who came to him.*

Who brought their children to Jesus?

Who tried to send the children away?

What did Jesus tell the disciples?

What did Jesus say is the only way to get into God's Kingdom?

What did Jesus do for the children?

STORY 94

# Zacchaeus Finds a Friend

LUKE 18:31-34; 19:1-10

One day Jesus told his twelve disciples that it was time to go to Jerusalem. He said that when they got there, everything the prophets had said about him would happen. (The writings of the prophets are in the part of the Bible that we now call the Old Testament.) Jesus said he would be laughed at and whipped. People would spit on him, put him on a cross, and kill him. But the third day he would come back to life.

The disciples thought Jesus was going to be crowned king of the Jews. So they couldn't understand what he was talking about.

When Jesus came to the city of Jericho on the way to Jerusalem, crowds of people followed him as they always did. A man named Zacchaeus lived in Jericho. He was in charge of collecting taxes in that city. And because he took more money from people than he should have, he was very rich.

As Jesus walked through the streets of the city, Zacchaeus tried to see him. But the crowd was too big and Zacchaeus was too short. So he ran ahead, climbed up into a tree beside the road, and waited for Jesus.

When Jesus came along the road that went past the tree, he stopped. He looked up into the branches and saw Zacchaeus. "Come down, Zacchaeus," Jesus told him. "I want to go to your house today!" So Zacchaeus climbed down. He was very happy to take Jesus home with him.

*Jesus looked up and said, "Come down, Zacchaeus."*

As soon as Zacchaeus began to talk with Jesus, he felt very sorry for the bad things he had done. He told Jesus that he would give half of his money to people who were poor. And if he had taken more money from people than he should, he would give them back four times as much!

Jesus saw that Zacchaeus was sorry and was ready to do what was right. So he told Zacchaeus that his sins were forgiven.

The people in the crowd were upset with Jesus for going to a sinner's house. But Jesus said that he had come into the world to look for sinners. He came to save them from being punished for their sins.

How did Zacchaeus get rich?

Why did Zacchaeus climb up into a tree?

What did Zacchaeus promise Jesus he would do with his money?

When Jesus saw that Zacchaeus was sorry, what did Jesus tell him?

STORY 95

# *Bartimaeus Wants to See*

MARK 10:46-52; LUKE 18:35-43

As Jesus and his disciples left Jericho, big crowds of people were still following them. A man named Bartimaeus was sitting beside the road, begging for money. He was blind. So when he heard a lot of noise, he couldn't see what was happening.

"Jesus of Nazareth is coming," someone told him.

As soon as Bartimaeus heard this, he began to shout. He said, "Jesus, please show that you care about me. Please help me!"

*Jesus told the blind man, "Because you have faith in me, you are well."*

212

"Be quiet!" some of the people told him.

But his shouts became louder. "Jesus, help me!"

As soon as Jesus heard him, he stopped. He said, "Tell that man to come to me."

So the people told Bartimaeus, "Jesus is calling for you!" The blind man jumped up, threw his coat to one side, and ran over to Jesus.

Then Jesus asked, "What do you want me to do for you?"

"Teacher, I want to see," the man answered.

"All right," Jesus told him. "Because you have faith in me, you are well."

Right away Bartimaeus could see! So he followed Jesus down the road. And he praised God for the wonderful miracle. Everyone who saw what happened praised God too.

**Where was Bartimaeus when Jesus came by?**

**When Jesus heard Bartimaeus calling for help, what did Jesus say?**

**What did Bartimaeus ask Jesus to do for him?**

**How did Bartimaeus show he was thankful for what Jesus did?**

STORY 96

# Jesus Eats Supper in Bethany

### JOHN 12:1-11

The Jewish people were getting ready for the Passover. This was a happy time to remember how God had helped his people leave Egypt many years before. A lot of people went to Jerusalem for the Passover each year.

Six days before the Passover, Jesus came to Bethany. Lazarus still lived there with his sisters. He was the man Jesus had brought back to life four days after he died.

Jesus and his disciples ate supper in Bethany with Mary, Martha, and Lazarus. While they were there, Mary took out a jar of perfume that cost a lot of money. She poured it over Jesus' feet and wiped his feet with her hair. The perfume made the whole house smell good.

But Judas was upset. "Why wasn't this perfume sold? The money could have been given to poor people," he said. But Judas didn't really care about poor people. He was the one who took care of the disciples' money, and he often took some of it for himself.

Jesus told him, "Leave Mary alone. She has done a good thing. You will always be able to help poor people, but I won't be here much longer."

*Mary knew that Jesus would not be with her much longer.*

Many people heard that Jesus was in town, so they came to see him. They also came to see Lazarus, because they knew Jesus had brought him back to life. The religious leaders were upset, because the people were following Jesus instead of them.

Why was the Passover such a special holiday?

Whom did Jesus eat supper with in Bethany?

What did Mary do for Jesus that pleased him?

Why did this upset Judas?

# *Jesus Rides a Colt*

MATTHEW 21:1-17; MARK 11:1-11;
LUKE 19:28-40; JOHN 12:12-19

Jesus left Bethany to go to Jerusalem. On the way, he sent two of his disciples to a nearby village. As they left, Jesus told them, "You'll see a donkey tied with her young colt, which has never been ridden. Untie the colt, and bring it to me. If anyone asks what you are doing, just say that the Lord needs it."

The disciples found the young donkey just as Jesus had said. And while they were untying it the owners asked, "What are you doing?"

"The Lord needs it," the disciples said. Then the owners let the two men have the donkey for Jesus to ride on. The disciples brought the young animal to Jesus and threw their coats across its back.

Jesus rode the donkey along the road to Jerusalem. As he did, many people in the crowd spread their coats on the road in front of him. Others cut down branches from the trees. They made

*People took palm branches and put them on the road for Jesus to ride over.*

215

a green carpet of palm branches for him to ride over. That is what people did when a king rode through their streets. The crowd around him began shouting, "Praise God for sending us a king!"

But Jesus knew that most of the people didn't really love him. In a few days they would be shouting, "Put him on a cross to die. Crucify him!"

When he came to Jerusalem, Jesus went up to the Temple and began healing people who were sick. He helped people who were blind and people who couldn't walk right. But the religious leaders were angry. They didn't like it when they heard some children at the Temple praising God for Jesus, and calling him their king. But Jesus was pleased and said, "God has taught the children to do this."

What did Jesus ask two disciples to find for him?

What did Jesus do with the young animal?

What were some ways that the people welcomed Jesus?

Who at the Temple praised God for sending Jesus?

STORY 98

# *Fixing Supper and Washing Feet*

### MATTHEW 26:17-19; MARK 14:12-16; LUKE 22:7-30; JOHN 13:1-17

It was now time to eat the special Passover supper. Peter and John asked Jesus where they should go to fix the Passover lamb and eat it.

"Go into Jerusalem," Jesus told them. "When you see a man carrying a jar of water, follow him into the house where he is going. Then say to the man who lives there, 'The Teacher wants to know where he can eat the Passover meal with his disciples.' The man will take you upstairs to a large room all set up for you. Fix the lamb there, and that is where we will eat it."

Peter and John did as Jesus said. Sure enough, they met a man with a jar of water. He took them to the room Jesus had told them about, and there they fixed the Passover meal.

In the evening Jesus came with his other disciples, and they all sat down for the supper. "I wanted very much to eat this Passover supper with you before my time comes to die," he told them. "I will not eat it again until I have given my life for you."

But the disciples didn't understand him, because they thought he was soon going to become king

*Jesus washed each of his disciples' feet and wiped them with a towel.*

of the Jews. They began to fight about which of them would be greatest in the Kingdom. Then Jesus told them, "In this world, rulers and other important people order others around. But with you it is different. The greatest of you should act like the least important. The one who wants to be the leader must be the servant of everyone!"

Jesus said, "I am your servant." Then he showed his disciples what he meant.

He got up from the table and put a towel around his waist. He poured water into a bowl and began to wash his disciples' feet. He wiped their feet with a towel. Then he came to Peter. But Peter didn't want Jesus to wash his feet, because he didn't think Jesus should be his servant. Jesus told him, "You don't understand now why I am doing it, but you will later."

"No," Peter told him. "I will not let you wash my feet."

Jesus said, "If I don't, you can't be my disciple. You won't belong to me!"

Peter said, "Then, Lord, don't wash just my feet. Wash my hands and my head, too!"

But Jesus told him, "That will not be necessary."

After Jesus had washed his disciples' feet, he came back to the table. He said, "Do you understand what I have done for you? You call me 'Teacher' and 'Lord.' And that is what I am. I have washed your feet. So you should follow my example and do as I have done to you."

........................................................................................

Where did Peter and John fix the Passover meal for Jesus and the disciples?

How did Jesus use water and a towel to show his disciples that he wanted to be their servant?

What did Jesus tell his disciples to do for each other?

........................................................................................

STORY 99

# Eating the Last Supper

MATTHEW 26:20-35; MARK 14:17-31; LUKE 22:14-34; JOHN 13:18-38; 17

As they ate the Passover supper, Jesus looked sad. He said to his disciples, "One of you eating with me will turn against me by handing me over to the religious leaders."

The disciples were surprised and sad to hear this. They looked at each other, wondering which one of them he was talking about. Peter pointed to the disciple sitting next to Jesus. So that disciple asked, "Lord, who will do such a terrible thing?"

"It is the one to whom I will give this piece of bread after I have dipped it in the dish," Jesus answered. Then he gave it to Judas and said, "Hurry. Go and do it now."

*Jesus broke apart a piece of bread and said, "This is my body, which is broken for you."*

Some of the disciples thought Jesus was telling Judas to go and buy some things they needed. Others thought that Judas was supposed to go and give some money to poor people.

After Judas left the room, Jesus said, "I will be with you only a little while longer. So I want to give you this new commandment: Love each other just as I have loved you. Everyone will know that you are my disciples because of your love for one another."

As they were eating, Jesus took a piece of bread and asked God to bless it. Then he broke it apart and gave it to his disciples to eat. "This is my body, which is broken for you," he told them. He meant that his body was soon to be broken when he was put on the cross to die for their sins.

Then Jesus thanked God for the wine and gave it to them. They all drank some of it as he said, "This wine is my blood. My blood will be shed so that God will forgive your sins."

While Jesus and his disciples sat at the supper table, he told them not to be sad that he was leaving them. He was going back to heaven to prepare places for them. Someday he would come again, and he would take everyone who loves him to be with him forever.

Then he looked up to heaven. He prayed for his disciples and for all those who would believe in him someday. He prayed that they would be safe from sin and that they would love one another.

After that, Jesus told his disciples they would all leave him that night. He said he would die, but then he would come back to life.

Peter told Jesus, "I will never leave you."

But Jesus said, "Peter, before the rooster crows tomorrow morning, you will say three times that you do not know me."

........................................................................

**What terrible thing did Jesus know that one of his disciples would do?**

**What was the new commandment Jesus gave his disciples?**

**What did Jesus and his disciples eat and drink at their last supper together?**

**What did Jesus tell Peter he would say three times?**

........................................................................

# Jesus Prays in a Garden

### MATTHEW 26:36-46; MARK 14:32-42; LUKE 22:39-46

Jesus and his disciples sang a song about God. Then they went out to the Mount of Olives, which wasn't far from Jerusalem. There they went into a garden called the garden of Gethsemane.

"Sit here while I go and pray," Jesus said. Then he went a little farther away and got down on his knees. "Dear Father," he prayed. "This is very hard for me. I don't want to die on the cross. But whatever you want, that is what I want too."

Jesus prayed so hard that he became very tired and sad. An angel came to keep him strong.

When Jesus went back to his disciples, he found them sleeping. "You're asleep?" he asked. "Get up and pray so that you won't give in and do something that's wrong." Then he went away and prayed again. When he came back he found them sleeping again. He went away a third time. When he returned he asked, "Are you still sleeping? Get up now, for the one who has turned against me is close by."

*Jesus prayed so hard that he became very tired and sad.*

What was the name of the garden where Jesus and his disciples went?

What did Jesus say in his prayer to God?

What did Jesus want his disciples to do instead of sleeping?

*When Judas kissed Jesus on the cheek, the other men grabbed Jesus.*

# Jesus Is Taken Away

MATTHEW 26:47-58, 69-75;
MARK 14:43-54, 66-72; LUKE 22:47-62;
JOHN 18:1-18, 25-27

Judas knew about the garden where Jesus went. So he told the religious leaders where it was, and they sent some men there with Judas.

Jesus knew that Judas was bringing the men to the garden, but he didn't run. He waited for them to come because it was time for him to die. While Jesus was still talking to his disciples, Judas and the others came. They were carrying swords and clubs and lanterns.

Judas had told the men, "The one I kiss on the cheek is the man you want." So Judas came up to Jesus and kissed him on the cheek the way men in Eastern lands do when they meet. Then the other men grabbed Jesus and held him.

"Lord, shall we use the sword?" the disciples cried out. Peter pulled out his sword and cut off the ear of a servant of the high priest.

"Put your sword away," Jesus told him. "If I wanted to, I could pray to my Father to send thousands of angels to save me. But I am to die for the people just as it is written in the Scriptures." Then Jesus touched the servant's ear and healed it.

Turning to the men holding him, Jesus asked, "Why the swords and clubs? If I have done something wrong, why didn't you come for me at the Temple? I was there every day."

Then all the disciples ran away.

The men took Jesus to the home of the high priest. All of the religious leaders were there.

Peter followed Jesus, but he didn't get too close. He sat down with the servants beside a fire in the courtyard.

A servant girl came over to him and said, "You were with Jesus of Galilee!" Peter lied and said, "No, I wasn't with him."

Then he went and stood by a gate. Another servant girl saw him there. She said to the others who were standing around, "This man was with Jesus of Nazareth!"

Again Peter lied. "I don't even know the man!" he said.

After a while another servant came to Peter. He was a relative of the man whose ear Peter had cut off. This servant said, "Didn't I see you with Jesus in the garden of Gethsemane?"

For the third time Peter said he didn't know Jesus. And right away he heard a rooster crow. Then he saw Jesus turn around and look at him.

Suddenly Peter remembered Jesus' words, "Before the rooster crows tomorrow morning, you will say three times that you do not know me." Then Peter felt terrible. He ran off, crying very hard.

**Who brought some men to the garden so they could take Jesus away?**

**Why didn't Jesus pray for angels to come and save him?**

**What did Peter remember when the rooster crowed?**

**Why did Peter cry as he ran away?**

STORY 102

# A Crown of Thorns

MATTHEW 26:59-68; 27:11-31;
MARK 14:55-65; 15:1-20; LUKE 22:63–23:25;
JOHN 18:28–19:16

Inside the high priest's house the religious leaders asked Jesus, "Are you telling us that you are the Son of God?"

Jesus said, "You are right. I am."

So the religious leaders took Jesus to Pilate, the Roman governor. But Pilate found nothing wrong with anything that Jesus had done. Pilate sent him to King Herod.

The king and his soldiers made fun of Jesus. They put a purple robe on him because he had said he was a king. Then Herod sent him back to Pilate.

Every year during the Passover, Pilate let one person out of jail that the people asked for. A man named Barabbas was in jail for killing someone. Pilate asked the people, "Whom shall I set free? Barabbas or Jesus?" He thought they would choose Jesus.

*Jesus was taken to Pilate, the Roman governor.*

But the crowd said to give them Barabbas. When Pilate asked what he should do with Jesus, everyone shouted, "Kill him! Put him on a cross. Crucify him!"

Pilate washed his hands, as if trying to clean himself from being blamed for killing Jesus. Then he told his soldiers to beat Jesus. They put a purple robe on him again and placed a crown of thorns on his head. It hurt a lot. They made fun of him and spit on him and hit him.

Then Pilate brought Jesus out to the religious leaders. "Take him yourselves and crucify him, for I find no reason for putting him to death," Pilate told them.

Soldiers took the purple robe off of Jesus and put his own clothes on him again. Then they led him away.

**What did Jesus say when the high priest asked if he was the Son of God?**

**How did the king and his soldiers make fun of Jesus?**

**Whom did the people choose when Pilate said he would let one prisoner go free?**

**Why did Pilate wash his hands?**

# The Cross

MATTHEW 27:32-54; MARK 15:21-39;
LUKE 23:26-47; JOHN 19:17-30

Jesus had to carry a heavy wooden cross to a place outside the city. But Jesus had no more strength, so he fell. Along the way a man named Simon was coming in from the country. When the soldiers saw him, they made him carry the cross. A crowd followed Jesus out to a place called The Skull, or Calvary. There the soldiers nailed Jesus' hands and feet to the cross.

Jesus prayed for those who hurt him and for those who told them to do it. "Father, forgive them, for they don't know what they are doing," he said. Jesus knew they didn't understand that he is the Son of God. They tried to give him a sour drink so he wouldn't feel the pain so much. But Jesus wouldn't drink it.

Two other men were hanging on crosses with Jesus. One was on his right side, and the other was on his left. Both of them had done many wrong things.

It was nine o'clock in the morning when the soldiers put Jesus on the cross. He hung there until three o'clock in the afternoon. The soldiers took his clothes and divided them up among themselves. Then they rolled dice to see who would get his coat.

Pilate told the soldiers to place a sign on the cross above Jesus' head. The sign said, "Jesus of Nazareth, the King of the Jews." The people passing by laughed and said, "If you are the Son of God, come down from the cross."

One of the men on a cross next to Jesus made fun of him. He said, "If you are the Christ, save yourself and us."

But the man on the other cross said, "Jesus, remember me when you come into your Kingdom."

*Jesus hung on a cross between two men who had done many wrong things.*

Jesus told the second man, "Today you will be with me in heaven." Jesus wanted the man to know that his sins were forgiven and that as soon as he died, he would go where Jesus was going.

Jesus saw his mother and his disciple John standing near the cross. He asked John to take care of his mother as if she were his own mother.

From noon until three in the afternoon there was darkness over all the land. God sent the darkness because wicked men were killing his Son.

At about three o'clock, Jesus called out with a loud voice, "My God, why have you left me?" God had turned away from him, and God had turned away from everyone's sins. Jesus was dying to take the punishment for those sins—those wrong things everyone does.

Then Jesus said he was thirsty. One of the men standing ran to get a sponge and filled it with sour wine. He held it up on a stick to Jesus' mouth so that he could drink it. Jesus tasted it. Then he cried out, "It is finished!" And he bowed his head and died.

At that very moment, the earth shook, rocks broke apart, and dead people who had loved God came out of their graves. When the Roman soldiers saw all of this, they were filled with fear. They said, "This really was the Son of God!"

Who helped Jesus carry his cross?

For whom did Jesus pray while he was on the cross?

Tell about the two men who were on crosses on each side of Jesus.

When Jesus died, what happened to make the soldiers believe he was God's Son?

# Jesus Comes Back to Life

MATTHEW 27:57–28:15
MARK 15:42–16:10; LUKE 23:50–24:12;
JOHN 19:31–20:18

When the soldiers saw that Jesus was dead, they stuck a spear into his side. Then everyone knew for sure that Jesus had died.

There was a garden nearby. And in the garden there was a new grave. It was a cave inside a rock, and it belonged to a rich man named Joseph of Arimathea.

Now Joseph went to Pilate and asked for Jesus' body. Pilate said Joseph could take it down and bury it. So Joseph took Jesus' body down from the cross. Nicodemus helped him wrap it in a long cloth. Then they laid it in the cave and rolled a huge stone across the door.

The Jewish leaders went to Pilate and said, "Sir, while Jesus was still alive, he said that after three days he would come back to life. Please send some men to seal up the tomb where he is buried. Have them stay until the third day. Then his disciples can't come at night to steal his body and tell everyone he has come back to life." So Pilate sent soldiers to guard the tomb.

Early on Sunday morning the angel of the Lord came down from heaven and rolled back the stone from the cave and sat upon it. His face was as bright as lightning, and his clothes were as white as snow. The soldiers shook with fear and fell down as if they were dead.

As it was getting light, Mary Magdalene and the other Mary and Salome began walking to the tomb. They were bringing spices to put on Jesus' body. "How can we ever roll the heavy stone away from the tomb?" they asked each other. But when they got there, the stone had already been rolled away! They went inside the cave, and they saw an angel in a white robe.

The angel surprised the women, and they were terribly afraid. But the angel said, "Don't be afraid. Are you looking for Jesus? He isn't here.

*When the women got to the tomb, the stone had already been rolled away!*

He has come back to life! See, that is where his body was. Now go and tell his disciples, including Peter, that he is alive again and will meet them in Galilee."

As the women ran from the cave, they were filled with fear. But they were also filled with joy. They hurried to find the disciples and give them the angel's message. But as they were running, Jesus met them. "Hello there!" he greeted them. They ran to him and held him by the feet and worshiped him. "Don't be afraid," he said. "Just go and tell my disciples to leave for Galilee, and they will see me there."

When Mary told Peter and John what the angel had said, they ran to the tomb to see for themselves that Jesus' body was gone. John got there first, but he didn't go into the cave. Then Peter came and went right inside the empty tomb. So then John went in too, and they finally knew that Jesus had really come back to life.

Some of the soldiers who had been at the tomb told the religious leaders what had happened during the night. The leaders gave them money so they would lie about it. The leaders told them, "Say that Jesus' disciples came during the night and stole Jesus' body."

So the soldiers took the money and told everyone what the religious leaders told them to say. But of course, it was a lie.

. . . . . . . . . . . . . . . . . . . . . . . . . . . . . . . . . . . . . . . . . . . . . . . . . . . . . . . . . . . . . . . . . . . . . . . . . . . . . . . .

What did Joseph and Nicodemus do with Jesus' body after he died?

When some women looked for Jesus in the tomb, what did they find instead?

As the women ran away from the cave, whom did they see, and what did he say?

What did Peter and John go to see for themselves?

. . . . . . . . . . . . . . . . . . . . . . . . . . . . . . . . . . . . . . . . . . . . . . . . . . . . . . . . . . . . . . . . . . . . . . . . . . . . . . . .

# Two Friends Walk to Emmaus

## MARK 16:12-14; LUKE 24:13-43; JOHN 20:19-23

Late that Sunday afternoon, two of Jesus' friends were walking to the village of Emmaus, which was about seven miles from Jerusalem. They were sad as they talked about all the things that had happened, because they didn't believe that Jesus really had come back to life.

Suddenly Jesus was there, walking along the road with them. But he looked different to them, so they didn't know who he was.

"What are you talking about that makes you so sad?" Jesus asked.

Cleopas answered, "You must be the only person in Jerusalem who hasn't heard about all the things that have happened the last few days."

"What things?" Jesus asked.

"The things that happened to Jesus of Nazareth," they said. "Our leaders had him nailed him to a cross three days ago, and he died.

"Early this morning some women who are followers of Jesus, just as we are, went to the cave where he was buried. They came back with the news that his body wasn't there. They said that some angels told them he is alive. Some of our men went to the tomb afterward and found it was true. Jesus' body wasn't there! But we don't understand what all of this means."

Then Jesus began to explain it to them. He said that everything written in the Scriptures (which were the first part of the Bible we have today) told about the Messiah who would be the Savior. The Scriptures said the Messiah would die for the people. But the friends Jesus was walking with didn't know he was talking about himself.

When they came to their village, the two friends invited Jesus to spend the night with them, since it was getting late in the day. So he went home with them.

As they sat down to eat supper together, Jesus took a small loaf of bread. After he had thanked God for it, he broke it and gave it to them. When he did this, suddenly his friends recognized him. But as soon as

*Suddenly Jesus was walking along the road with two of his friends!*

they knew, Jesus was gone! Then they said to each other, "Didn't you feel good inside while he was talking with us out there on the road, explaining God's Word?"

They started back to Jerusalem, where they found Jesus' disciples and his other followers. The two from Emmaus told how they had seen Jesus and talked with him, and how they knew who he was when he broke the bread at the supper table. Just as they were telling about it, Jesus himself suddenly came and stood right there with them! The disciples were all afraid, because they thought they were seeing a ghost!

Then Jesus said to them, "Look at the nail marks in my hands and feet. Touch me, and you'll know that I'm not a ghost, for a ghost doesn't have a body."

Jesus' followers were full of joy, but they could hardly believe what was happening!

"Do you have anything here to eat?" Jesus asked. They gave him some fish and watched him eat it. Jesus was no ghost. He was real, and he was alive.

..........................................................................................

Why were Jesus' two friends from Emmaus sad?

What did Jesus do with a loaf of bread that showed his two friends who he was?

How did Jesus help his disciples understand that he was not a ghost?

..........................................................................................

STORY 106

# Thomas Believes

JOHN 20:24-29

One of the disciples, whose name was Thomas, wasn't with the other disciples that first Sunday evening, the day when Jesus came back to life. So Thomas didn't get to see Jesus. The others told him afterward that Jesus is alive.

But Thomas said, "I won't believe it unless I see him and touch the nail marks in Jesus' hands. I also need to touch the spear wound in his side. I won't believe Jesus is alive unless I can do those things."

A week later the disciples were again meeting together behind locked doors. This time Thomas was with them too. Suddenly Jesus was standing there among them, just like the last time! He said, "Peace be with you." Then he said to Thomas, "Put your finger on the nail marks in my hands. And place your hand on my side where the spear went. Then believe."

Thomas needed only to see Jesus and hear his voice to believe that it really was Jesus, and that he was alive. Thomas also knew then that Jesus is God's Son. He said, "My Lord and my God!"

"Thomas," Jesus said to him, "you did not believe until you saw me. But blessed are those who believe even though they haven't seen me."

*Thomas said, "I won't believe Jesus is alive until I see him."*

Which disciple did not see Jesus the same day he came back to life?

What did Thomas say he needed to do before he could believe Jesus had come back to life?

A week later, when Thomas was with the others, what did Jesus say to him?

What did Thomas say to Jesus that shows he knew who Jesus was?

What does Jesus want us to do even though we can't see him?

# Breakfast with Jesus

### JOHN 21:1-17

One day after Jesus came back to life, he found some of his disciples fishing in a boat out on the Sea of Galilee. This is the way it happened.

When Peter said he was going out to fish, Thomas, Nathanael, James, John, and two other disciples said they would go along. They did, but they caught nothing all night. Early the next morning Jesus was standing on the shore, but the disciples couldn't see who he was.

"Did you catch any fish?" he asked them.

"No," they said.

"Throw your net out on the right side of the boat, and you'll catch plenty of fish!" Jesus told them.

They did what he said, and soon the net was so full of fish that they couldn't drag it back into the boat! John said, "It's the Lord." When Peter heard him say that, he jumped right into the water and began swimming to Jesus. The others followed and brought the net full of fish to the shore.

As soon as they came to land, they saw a fire burning. Fish were frying over it, and there was bread.

"Bring some of the fish you caught," said Jesus. So Peter went back for the fish. There were 153 big ones, but the net did not break!

"Come and have breakfast," Jesus called.

After breakfast, Jesus asked Peter, "Do you love me?"

*Jesus cooked breakfast for his disciples.*

236

Peter answered, "Yes, Lord, you know that I love you."

Jesus asked the same question three times, and each time Peter said, "Yes."

Then Jesus said to Peter, "Take care of my followers. They are my sheep."

..........................................................................

Who helped the disciples catch the fish, just as he had done another time?

What did Jesus serve the disciples for breakfast?

After breakfast by the lake, what did Jesus ask Peter three times?

How did Peter answer Jesus each time?

..........................................................................

STORY 108

# Jesus Returns to Heaven

MATTHEW 28:16-20; MARK 16:15-20; LUKE 24:44-53; ACTS 1:1–2:41; 1 CORINTHIANS 15:3-8

The eleven disciples went to a mountain in Galilee, where Jesus had said they should meet him. When they saw him, they worshiped him. He told them, "God has given me all power in heaven and on earth. Go and preach the Good News to the people of every nation. Baptize them in the name of the Father, the Son, and the Holy Spirit. And teach them to obey all the commands I have given you."

The disciples were not the only ones who saw Jesus after he came back to life. One time, more than five hundred people saw him!

Forty days after he came back to life, Jesus came to the disciples in Jerusalem again. He told them, "Stay here until I send you the Holy Spirit. He will fill you with power from God in heaven."

*While Jesus was blessing the disciples, he began to rise into the air.*

Then Jesus walked with them to a place near the village of Bethany. And while he was blessing them, he began to rise into the air until he went behind a cloud and no one could see him anymore!

While the disciples stood there trying to see him, two angels came. They were dressed in white. The angels said, "Why stand here looking at the sky? Jesus has gone to heaven. But he will return someday, just as you have seen him go."

So Jesus' followers returned to Jerusalem. They went there to wait until the Holy Spirit came.

Just ten days later, the disciples were meeting together when suddenly they heard a sound from heaven. It was like the roar of a strong wind. Then something that looked like small flames or tongues of fire sat on each of their heads. That's when the Holy Spirit filled them with God's power. After that, they all began to speak in languages that people from other countries could understand. Peter told the people about Jesus, and about three thousand people believed in the Lord Jesus that day and were baptized.

When Jesus met his disciples on a mountain, what job did he give them?

What does the picture show Jesus doing?

Who told the disciples that Jesus had gone to heaven?

What did Peter do when the Holy Spirit filled him and the other disciples with God's power?

# Philip Has Good News for a Man from Ethiopia

### ACTS 6:1-7; 8:4-8, 26-40

A man named Philip was one of seven men chosen for a special job. These men helped poor widows get the food and money they needed. Philip and his friends worked hard at their job. This gave the disciples more time to preach. Then more and more people became followers of Jesus.

Before long, God had more work for Philip to do. Philip went to the city of Samaria and preached the Good News about Jesus. Then an angel of the Lord told Philip to leave Samaria and go south to a desert road between Jerusalem and Gaza. He obeyed, but he didn't know what he was to do when he got there.

As he was walking along the dusty road, Philip met a man from the land of Ethiopia riding in a nice carriage. He was a very important man in his country, because he took care of everything that belonged to the queen. He had been in Jerusalem to worship at the Temple. And now as he was going home to Ethiopia, he was reading what the prophet Isaiah had written. He was reading the part where Isaiah said that a Savior was coming into the world to die for everyone's sins.

*The man from Ethiopia asked Philip about the words that a prophet wrote.*

The Holy Spirit told Philip to go over to the carriage and talk with the man. When Philip ran over there, he heard the man reading aloud.

"Do you understand what you are reading?" Philip called out to him.

"How can I understand it unless someone explains it to me?" the man said. Then he asked Philip to come and sit with him in the carriage to talk about it.

As they rode along, the man from Ethiopia asked Philip about Isaiah's words. "What did the prophet mean when he wrote that someone would be taken away like a sheep to be killed? Was he talking about himself or someone else?"

Philip explained that Isaiah was talking about Jesus. Then he went on to tell more of the Good News about Jesus.

After a while they came to a pool of water beside the road.

The Ethiopian man said, "Look! There is some water! Can't I be baptized?" He wanted this because he believed that Jesus is the Son of God. The man ordered his carriage to stop, and he and Philip went down into the water. Then Philip baptized him.

When they came out again, suddenly Philip was gone. The Holy Spirit took him away! But the Ethiopian man went home happy because now he believed in Jesus and was one of his followers.

What was Philip's first special job?

When Philip was in Samaria, where did an angel of the Lord send him?

Did the Ethiopian man understand what he was reading?

What did Philip explain to the man?

What did the man ask Philip to do when they came to a pool of water?

# A Light from Heaven Makes Saul Blind

### ACTS 8:3; 9:1-9

Saul of Tarsus did not believe in Jesus. He went everywhere, looking for Jesus' followers so he could put them in jail or kill them. He asked the high priest in Jerusalem to write letters to the religious leaders in the city of Damascus. He wanted the leaders to help him find people there who were followers of Jesus. Then he would bring them back to Jerusalem, where they would be sent to jail for believing that Jesus came to be the Savior of the world.

The high priest gave Saul the letters he wanted. So he left for Damascus. But as he came near the city, a bright light from heaven suddenly began to shine around him. Saul fell down to the ground as he heard a voice saying, "Saul, Saul, why are you trying to hurt me?"

Saul asked, "Who are you, sir?"

The voice answered, "I am Jesus, the one you are hurting. Now get up and go into Damascus. Someone there will tell you what to do next."

The men who were with Saul didn't know what to say. They heard the voice but couldn't understand the words.

When Saul got up, he found out that he couldn't see a thing. Those who were with him had to lead him to Damascus. For three days he was blind, and he didn't eat or drink anything. He just waited as Jesus had told him to do. He waited to learn what would happen next.

---

**Why was Saul going to Damascus?**

**What happened on the way that made Saul change his mind?**

**What did Saul do in Damascus for three days?**

---

*A bright light shone from heaven, and Saul fell to the ground.*

# Saul Can See Again

### ACTS 9:10-28

Ananias, who lived in Damascus, believed in the Lord Jesus. The Lord said to him, "Go to Straight Street and ask at the house of Judas for a man named Saul. He is praying to me right now, and I have let him see in his mind that you will come to him. I have shown him that you will put your hands on him and he will be able to see again!"

Ananias said, "Lord, I have heard about all the terrible things this man has done to the people in Jerusalem who believe in you. And now he has come to Damascus to have your followers here put in jail."

But the Lord said, "Go and do what I say. I want Saul to preach my Good News to kings and Jewish people and others, too. I want him to tell everyone about me."

So Ananias found Saul and placed his hands on him. He said, "Brother Saul, the Lord Jesus came to you along the road to Damascus. Now he has sent me here to help you see and so that you will be filled with the Holy Spirit."

Right away Saul's eyes could see again. He got up and was baptized. Then he ate and felt strong again. Saul stayed with the people who believed in Jesus. He went into the synagogues, where the Jewish people worshiped God. There Saul preached to the Jews, telling them, "Jesus really is the Son of God!"

The people could hardly believe what they heard!

"Isn't this the man who made things hard for Jesus' followers in

*Saul went back to Jerusalem and looked for Jesus' followers.*

244

Jerusalem?" they asked. "And he came here to take people who believe in Jesus back with him in chains."

Saul kept preaching. He helped the Jews see that Jesus came to be the Savior. But the Jewish leaders didn't want the people to believe. They began to talk about killing Saul. So one night Jesus' followers helped Saul by putting him in a large basket and letting him down through a hole in the city wall.

When Saul went back to Jerusalem, he looked for Jesus' followers. He no longer wanted to hurt them, but they were afraid of him. They couldn't believe he had really become one of them. Then Barnabas, who was one of Jesus' followers, brought Saul to the disciples and told them everything was all right. He told them Saul had met Jesus on the road to Damascus.

After that, Jesus' disciples let Saul stay with them. He was with them all the time, preaching in Jerusalem.

Why was Ananias afraid to help Saul at first?

What happened when Ananias placed his hands on Saul?

How did Saul get out of Damascus when some leaders wanted to kill him?

Who told Jesus' followers in Jerusalem not to be afraid of Saul?

STORY 112

# The Good News Is for Everyone

ACTS 9:32–10:48

Jesus' disciple Peter went from place to place, visiting Jesus' followers. He stayed in the town of Joppa for a long time and lived at the home of Simon, a man who made things from leather. During that time, an angel told a man named Cornelius about Peter.

*Peter baptized Cornelius in the name of Jesus.*

Cornelius, who lived in the city of Caesarea, was an officer in the Roman army. Even though he wasn't Jewish, he taught his family about God. He gave many gifts to poor people, and he prayed to God often.

One afternoon God let Cornelius see an angel coming toward him. Cornelius was afraid. "What do you want, sir?" he asked.

The angel answered, "God has heard your prayers, and he has seen your gifts to poor people. Now send men to Joppa to find Peter, a man who is staying by the sea in Simon's house. Ask him to come and see you."

So Cornelius sent two servants and a soldier to Joppa to find Peter.

The next day Peter went up to the flat roof of Simon's house to pray. As he was praying, the sky above him seemed to open. In his mind God showed him something like a large sheet coming down. On this sheet were all kinds of wild animals and snakes and birds. A voice said, "Kill them and eat them, Peter."

Peter said he couldn't do that. He was thinking about the laws that God had given to Moses many years before. The laws said that God's people could not eat those kinds of animals, snakes, and birds.

Then Peter heard the voice again. "When God says it is all right, don't say it isn't!"

This happened three times.

Just then the three men sent by Cornelius came to the house where Peter was staying. The Holy Spirit said to Peter, "Three men are looking for you. Don't be afraid to go with them, for I have sent them."

So Peter went down to the men and asked them to stay there that night. The next day he went with them to Caesarea, and some of Jesus' other followers went along.

Cornelius, his family, and some good friends were waiting for them. As Peter walked into the house, Cornelius got down on his knees and started to worship him. But Peter said, "Stand up! I am only a man like you!"

Then Peter said to the people inside, "You know about the laws of the Jewish people. Those laws say it is wrong for Jews to visit people like you who aren't Jewish. But God has let me see that it's all right."

Then Peter said, "I understand now that God doesn't love people from one nation more than another. In every country there are people who worship God and do what is right. God lets them be part of his family.

"God sent Jesus into the world, and he went around doing good. Then the religious leaders put him on a cross to die. But God brought him back to life on the third day and let many of us see him. Jesus will forgive the sins of all who believe in him."

While Peter was speaking, the Holy Spirit came to Cornelius, his family, and his friends. Peter asked the Jewish friends who came with him, "Shouldn't they be baptized? They have received the Holy Spirit just as we have."

So Cornelius and the others were baptized in the name of Jesus. Then they asked Peter to stay with them for several days.

Who was Cornelius?

What good things did Cornelius do that pleased God?

An angel told Cornelius to find someone. Who was it?

As Peter prayed on a flat roof, what did he see in his mind?

What did Peter tell the people at Cornelius's house about God's love?

*Suddenly the prison was full of light, and an angel stood by Peter!*

# An Angel Gets Peter Out of Jail

### ACTS 12:1-17

King Herod began to make trouble for the Christians in Jerusalem. He put Peter in jail and placed soldiers all around him. They guarded him night and day so that he couldn't get away. But the church in Jerusalem kept praying for him.

The night before Peter was to be taken to court, he was sleeping between two soldiers. He was chained to the soldiers, so they could tell if he moved even a little bit.

Suddenly the prison was full of light, and an angel was standing there! He tapped Peter on the side to wake him up. "Quick, get up!" he said. The soldiers kept sleeping as the chains fell off Peter's hands. "Dress yourself and put on your shoes," the angel said to him. "Now put on your coat and follow me."

Peter did this, but he thought it was only a dream. After they passed the guards and came to the iron gate that led out of the jail, the gate opened by itself. They started walking down the street, but suddenly the angel was gone.

Then Peter understood that it wasn't a dream. He said to himself, "It's true! The Lord sent his angel to save me!" Then he went to the home of Mary, who had a son named Mark. Many Christians were there, praying for Peter. He knocked at the door in the gate, and a girl named Rhoda came to open it. But when she heard Peter's voice, she was so happy that she forgot to let him in. All she could think of doing was running back to tell everyone that Peter was at the door!

"You don't know what you're saying!" they told her. "Peter is in jail!" But she told them he really was at the door.

"Then it must be his angel," they said.

Peter kept on knocking. The people were surprised when they finally opened the door and saw Peter there! After he got them to quiet down, he told them what had happened. He asked them to tell his other friends about it too. Then he left.

Who put Peter in jail?

How did Peter get out of jail?

What were many Christians doing at Mary's house?

What did Jesus' followers say when Rhoda told them Peter was at the door?

When did the people know for sure that God had answered their prayers?

STORY 114

# *Saul Becomes Paul, the Missionary*

ACTS 11:20-26; 13–14; 15:36–16:5

Some of Jesus' followers in the city of Antioch began preaching to people who weren't Jews. And God helped many of those people believe in his Son, Jesus.

When the church in Jerusalem heard about this, they sent Barnabas to Antioch. Barnabas was a good man who was full of faith and the Holy Spirit. While he was in Antioch, many more people believed in Jesus.

Then Barnabas went to the city of Tarsus. He found Saul there and brought him back to Antioch. The two of them stayed there a whole year, preaching the Good News. (It was in Antioch that people who believed in Jesus were first called Christians.)

One day the Holy Spirit told some of the Christians at Antioch to send Barnabas and Saul to other countries. They would preach the Good News to people everywhere. The Christians placed their hands on the heads of Barnabas and Saul to bless them. And they sent them away as missionaries.

Barnabas and Saul sailed first to the island of Cyprus. They took Mark with them as their helper.

On the island they met a Jewish man who didn't want them to preach about Jesus. Saul, who was also called Paul, told the man that the Lord would make him blind for a while. And right away everything looked dark to the man. Because of that, the governor of the island believed in Jesus.

Then Paul and his friends sailed to the land north of Cyprus, but Mark went back to Jerusalem. Paul and Barnabas came to a city where there was a Jewish synagogue. They went into this worship place to teach.

Paul told how God had set the people of Israel free when they were slaves in Egypt. And he shared the Good News that Jesus is the Savior. "All of your sins will be forgiven if you believe in him."

The next week almost the entire city came to hear Paul and Barnabas. But the Jewish leaders were upset. They wanted the people to follow them, not Jesus. So they said bad things about Paul and his message.

*Paul preached the Good News to people everywhere.*

Paul and Barnabas told the Jews, "Since you don't want to hear the Good News, we will preach it to everyone else. We'll tell all the Gentiles about Jesus, for that is what God has told us to do." They said that Jesus is the Savior of all the nations. Everyone was happy to hear this except the Jewish leaders. They ran Paul and Barnabas out of town.

In the next city, the people became angry and were ready to stone Paul and Barnabas to death. So the missionaries ran to another city. A man who had never walked believed that Jesus could make him well. Paul shouted, "Stand up!" Then the man jumped up and walked! All the people started to worship Paul and Barnabas. But the two men said, "We are just people like you. We want you to worship the true living God, who made heaven and earth."

Some Jewish people came from towns that the missionaries had already visited. They got everyone upset. So now, instead of worshiping Paul and Barnabas, the people tried to kill them. They stoned Paul and dragged him out of the city.

But Paul and Barnabas kept traveling. And they chose leaders for the new churches in each city where they had been. Finally they went back to Antioch to talk about their trip.

After a while, the two missionaries went back to visit the new churches. Barnabas took Mark with him and sailed to the island of Cyprus. Paul took Silas with him. In one of the towns Paul asked a young man named Timothy to go along with him and Silas. As they traveled from town to town, they helped many more people believe in Jesus.

Where were Jesus' followers first called Christians?

Who were the first two missionaries?

Whom did some Jewish leaders want the people to follow instead of Jesus?

STORY 115

# An Earthquake Shakes a Jail

ACTS 16:12, 16-40

In the city of Philippi, Paul and Silas met a slave girl who had an evil spirit in her. The evil spirit helped her know about things that hadn't happened yet. So people paid her to tell them what was going to happen to them. She earned a lot of money for her masters that way.

The girl followed Paul and his friends and shouted, "These men are servants of God. They will tell you how to be saved." This went on for several days.

Paul didn't like to hear an evil spirit talk about Jesus. At last he turned around and said to the spirit inside the girl, "In the name of Jesus Christ, come out of her." And right away the spirit came out and left her.

Her masters were angry. Now the girl could no longer earn money for them by telling people what was going to happen. The men grabbed Paul and Silas, took them to the city leaders, and told lies about them. "These Jews are getting everyone in our city upset," they shouted. "They are teaching the people to do things that are against our Roman laws."

A crowd of people became angry with Paul and Silas. So the city leaders gave an order for the men to get a beating. After that, Paul and Silas were put in jail. The jailer, the man who was in charge of the jail, was told to be sure they didn't get out. So he took them into a room way inside the prison and put their feet through holes in some blocks of wood, locking them in place.

In the middle of the night Paul and Silas were praying and singing praises to God. Suddenly a great earthquake shook the whole jail. All the doors opened, and everyone's chains fell off! The jailer woke up and thought everyone had run away. He was ready to kill himself, because he was afraid that he would be killed anyway for letting the prisoners escape. But Paul shouted to him, "Don't hurt yourself. We are all here."

Then the man called for a light and ran into the room where Paul and Silas were. He got down on his knees and cried out, "Sirs, what must I do to be saved?"

They answered him, "Believe in the Lord Jesus, and you will be saved. Your family will believe and be saved too." When they told him and his family about the Savior, they all believed and were baptized.

Paul and Silas had received a bad beating, so the jailer washed the blood from their backs. He even gave them a meal in his own house. How happy he and his family were to believe in Jesus!

In the morning the city leaders sent some officers to tell the jailer, "Let those men go."

*The jailer cried out to Paul and Silas, "Sirs, what must I do to be saved?"*

So the jailer told Paul and Silas they could leave. But Paul said, "The city leaders had no right to beat us. Even though we are Roman citizens, they put us in jail without taking us to court to be judged. If they want us to leave, let them send us away themselves."

When the city leaders heard that Paul and Silas were Roman citizens, the leaders came and said they were sorry. Then they asked the two men to leave.

Name the two men whom a slave girl's masters told lies about.

Where were the two missionaries put?

What were they doing in the middle of the night when an earthquake came?

How did Paul and Silas help the jailer and his family?

STORY 116

# Paul Goes Back to Jerusalem

### ACTS 20:13–23:11

Paul and his friends sailed to a place near Ephesus. Paul was in a hurry to get to Jerusalem. So he sent for the leaders of the Ephesian church to meet him by the boat.

When they came he said to them, "I stayed with you three years. I taught in the synagogue and in your own homes, telling both Jews and Gentiles that they must be sorry for their sins and believe in the Lord Jesus Christ.

"And now I am going to Jerusalem. I don't know what will happen to me there. But wherever I go, the Holy Spirit keeps telling me that jail and other bad things will be waiting for me. It doesn't matter, though. The only thing that's important to me is that I keep telling others the Good News about Jesus."

*The Ephesian church leaders met Paul by the ship.*

Then Paul said, "I know that none of you will ever see me again." When he got down on his knees to pray with the church leaders, they all cried together. They felt sad as they hugged him for the last time. Then they went with him to the ship and watched him sail away.

Paul went to the city of Tyre and stayed there seven days. Then he and his friends sailed on to the city of Caesarea.

Finally Paul and his friends went to Jerusalem, where the church gave them a warm welcome. Then Paul went to the Temple. While he was there, some Jews from the area known as Asia saw him. They shouted, "Men of Israel, help! This man teaches people that they don't need to obey Jewish laws. He even brings Gentiles into the Temple!"

Soon the whole city was upset. A mob pulled Paul out of the Temple, trying to kill him. But as they were doing it, someone told the captain of the Roman army.

The captain took some of his soldiers with him and ran down among the people. When the men who were beating Paul saw the soldiers, they stopped. Then the captain took him away and gave an order to put chains on Paul. As he was being carried up some stairs, the crowd followed him, shouting, "Kill him!"

After the soldiers took Paul away, Jesus talked to Paul during the night. He said, "Don't be afraid, Paul. You have told the people here in Jerusalem about me, and now you must also preach about me in the city of Rome."

................................................................

Who met Paul by a boat?

What did Paul say was the only thing that was important to him?

Before he left for Jerusalem, what did Paul and the people do together?

When a mob tried to kill Paul, how did a Roman army captain help him?

................................................................

STORY 117

# Paul's Nephew Saves His Life

ACTS 23:12–25:12

The morning after soldiers took Paul away, more than forty Jews promised one another not to eat or drink until they had killed Paul. Then they told their leaders about the promise. They said, "We want you to have the captain bring Paul back to you tomorrow. Tell him you want to ask Paul some more questions. But before he gets to you, we will kill him."

Paul's nephew heard about their plan and went to tell Paul. Then Paul called one of the officers and said, "Take this young man to the captain. He has something to tell him."

So the officer took Paul's nephew to the captain of the Roman army. The young man told him, "Some of the Jews are going to ask you to take Paul to their leaders again tomorrow. But don't do it. More than forty of them will be hiding along the road, waiting to kill him."

"Don't let anyone know you told me this," the captain said. Then he sent Paul's nephew away.

Right away the captain made plans to send Paul to Felix, the Roman governor of Judea. Felix lived by the sea in the city of Caesarea. The captain told two of his officers to get 470 soldiers ready to go to Caesarea that night. He said that 70 of them were to ride horses and 200 were to have spears. "Have horses ready for Paul to ride, and get him safely to the governor."

Then the captain wrote this letter to Governor Felix: "Some of the Jews wanted to kill the man I am sending you. I had my soldiers keep him safe, because I heard he was a Roman. I have told the Jews to go to you and tell you what he has done that is wrong."

So the soldiers left that night with Paul. The next day they brought him and the letter to the governor, who had Paul put in jail.

Five days later the high priest and some of the council came from Jerusalem to Caesarea, bringing a lawyer with them.

They told the governor, "We have found that this man makes trouble wherever he goes. He is a leader among those who believe in Jesus of Nazareth, and he took Gentiles into the Temple! If you talk to him yourself, you'll find out that all of these things are true."

Paul told the governor, "It was only twelve days ago that I went to Jerusalem to worship at the Temple, but I didn't make trouble or stir up the people.

"I do worship God in a different way than the Jewish people do, for I believe in Jesus. But I also believe the Jewish laws and the words that the prophets have written. And just like these Jewish men, I believe

*Paul's nephew told Paul about a plan to kill him.*

that everyone will come back to life someday. So I always try to do what pleases God."

Governor Felix told the soldiers to keep Paul in jail but to let his friends visit him. A few days later Felix sent for Paul to come and talk with him and his wife. Paul talked to them about Jesus. For two years Felix often sent for Paul and talked with him.

Then Festus became the governor. He asked Paul if he would mind going back to Jerusalem to be judged. But Paul said he wanted to be judged by Caesar in Rome. Caesar was the emperor over all Romans everywhere.

Whom did Paul's nephew tell about the plan to kill Paul?

How many soldiers took Paul to see Governor Felix in Caesarea?

What did Paul tell the governor he believed?

STORY 118

# Shipwrecked but Safe

ACTS 27; 28:11-14

When the time came for Paul to be sent to Rome, an army captain named Julius was put in charge of him and several other prisoners. They went by ship from Caesarea. When they reached Fair Havens on the island of Crete, it was almost winter. That was the time for storms. So Paul said to the ship's officers, "If we keep going, the ship and our lives will be in great danger."

The captain of the ship didn't believe Paul. So he headed for a seaport called Phoenix, a good place to stay for the winter. The wind blew softly from the south that day, so everyone except Paul felt good about leaving.

But soon a storm came. The wind beat against the ship until the sailors couldn't steer it any longer. They had to let the ship go where the wind blew it. As they came near a small island, the sailors put ropes

*When the boat crashed, the men who could not swim hung on to boards from the boat.*

around the ship to keep it from breaking to pieces. The storm grew worse, and the next day the sailors threw out some of the cargo—things they were taking with them. They wanted to make the ship lighter to keep it from sinking.

The storm kept on day after day, with dark clouds covering the sky. At last the men gave up hope, thinking they would all die. They hadn't eaten anything for many days.

Then Paul stood up and said, "Men, you should have listened to me and stayed at Fair Havens. But don't be afraid. No one will die even though the ship will go down. I know this is true because last night God sent an angel. He told me, 'Don't be afraid. You will get to Rome safely and be judged by Caesar. And God is good, for he will save the lives of everyone in this ship.'

"So cheer up," Paul said. "I believe God, and I believe what the angel told me. We will be safe, but our ship will be wrecked on an island."

Two weeks after the storm started, the sailors could tell that they were near land. They dropped a line with a heavy weight and found that the water was 120 feet deep. A little later they found it was only 90 feet deep. They let four anchors down into the water to keep the ship from being driven onto nearby rocks. Then they prayed for daylight.

When morning came, Paul told everyone on the boat, "You haven't eaten in two weeks. Please take some food, and don't worry. No one will be hurt." Then he took some bread, thanked God for it in front of everyone, and began to eat. Suddenly everyone else felt better, and all 276 people began eating.

The next morning the men saw the shore with a sandy beach. They cut off the anchors and put the sail up, trying to head the ship toward the shore between the rocks. But before they reached land, the ship ran into some sand at the bottom of the sea. The front part of the ship got stuck, while the back part broke apart when high waves crashed against it.

The soldiers wanted to kill the prisoners instead of letting them get away. But the captain wanted to save Paul and wouldn't let them do it. He told everyone who could swim to jump into the water and swim to shore. He told the others to hang on to boards from the ship. So everyone reached land safely.

For three months the ship's captain stayed with Paul and the other prisoners on the island where the boat had crashed. Then they found another ship and sailed to a city near Rome and walked the rest of the way.

Why did Paul tell the ship's officers to keep the ship in Fair Havens?

What did an angel tell Paul during the storm?

What happened to the ship when it came near land?

What happened to the people on the ship?

# Dressed like Soldiers for God

ACTS 28:16; EPHESIANS 4:1, 17-32; 5:21–6:4; 6:10-18; PHILIPPIANS 4:4-7; COLOSSIANS 3:16-17

While Paul was a prisoner in Rome, he lived in a house with a soldier guarding him. And he wrote letters to churches.

One letter was to the Ephesian Christians—the Christians who lived in Ephesus. Paul wrote about things that are helpful to all people who love Jesus. He said, "You must be new people, holy and good like God. You must never lie to each other. And if you are angry, don't let yourself keep feeling that way. Put a stop to it before the sun goes down."

Then Paul said to work and earn money to share with poor people. He said, "Be kind to each other, and care about everyone. Forgive one another, just as God has forgiven you because you belong to Christ."

Paul told how a happy family can please God. The wife should let her husband lead her in the same way that she lets Jesus lead her. The husband should love his wife the same way that Christ loved the church— enough to die for it! And what should the children do? They should obey their parents. Why? One of God's Ten Commandments says, "If you honor your father and mother, you will live a long life filled with God's gifts and care." Paul also said fathers should show love and kindness as they teach their children to do what's right.

Then Paul told how everyone can get ready to fight the devil, also known as Satan. The devil is our enemy. So Paul wrote about dressing like a soldier to fight him.

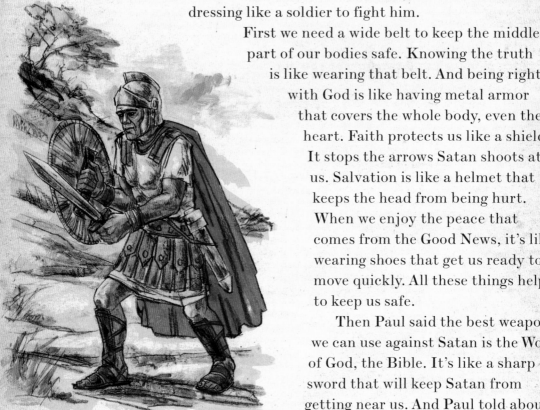

First we need a wide belt to keep the middle part of our bodies safe. Knowing the truth is like wearing that belt. And being right with God is like having metal armor that covers the whole body, even the heart. Faith protects us like a shield. It stops the arrows Satan shoots at us. Salvation is like a helmet that keeps the head from being hurt. When we enjoy the peace that comes from the Good News, it's like wearing shoes that get us ready to move quickly. All these things help to keep us safe.

Then Paul said the best weapon we can use against Satan is the Word of God, the Bible. It's like a sharp sword that will keep Satan from getting near us. And Paul told about one more good way to win the battle with Satan: Pray all the time!

*Everyone can get ready to fight the devil.*

Paul also talked about prayer in a letter to the believers in Philippi, the city where Paul was once in prison with Silas. Paul wrote to the Philippians, "Always be full of joy in the Lord. I say it again—rejoice! Let everyone see how kind you are. And remember that Jesus is coming back soon, so don't worry about anything. Instead, pray about everything. Tell God what you need, and don't forget to thank him for what he has already done." Paul promised that people who do this will have God's peace, which is more wonderful than anyone's mind can understand.

There was another group of believers in the city of Colosse. In his letter to the Colossians, Paul wrote, "Remember Jesus' words. Let them make you wise. Use his words to teach each other, and sing worship songs to God. Let everything you say and do show other people what Jesus is like."

What did Paul write about ways families can please God?

Name some things we can use to keep us safe as we fight the devil.

What did Paul tell the Philippians to do instead of worrying?

What did Paul say the Colossians should do with Jesus' words?

STORY 120

# A Letter That Wasn't Signed

### HEBREWS 9–13

One of the letters in the New Testament is not signed. Paul may have written it, or maybe Luke or Barnabas did. Or maybe it was someone else. It doesn't really matter. What's important is that it was written to help Hebrew Christians and all of us understand that no one is as special as Jesus.

The writer tells us that Jesus Christ is like the high priest of the Old Testament. The high priest could go into the Most Holy Place in the Temple. He took with him the blood from animals that people had given as gifts to God. Then God would forgive the sins of the priest and the other people.

But after Jesus came and died to become our Savior, animals were no longer needed as gifts to God. Jesus died just one time to give his own

*Life is like running a race.*

blood and take away our sins. Now we know that when he comes back, everyone who is waiting for him will be able to live with him forever.

Because Jesus, our Savior, is also the High Priest now, we can talk to God anytime. We can trust him and talk to him in prayer.

Faith in Jesus makes us sure we are saved. What is faith? It's being sure something is going to happen, even though we can't see it happening now. We sometimes hope and dream about something we wish would happen. But that isn't really faith. Faith is being just as certain of something as if we could see it now.

Then the writer of the letter to the Hebrews lists many people whose lives showed they had the great gift of faith. As you have been reading this book of Bible stories, you have read about these people. So you know about the ways they served God. The letter says that some of the people who had faith in God were Abel, Enoch, Noah, Abraham, Sarah, Jacob, and Joseph. Then there were Moses and his parents, the Israelites who followed Moses out of Egypt, and the soldiers who marched around Jericho. The writer also talks about Rahab, Gideon, Samson, David, Samuel, and many others who believed in God and had faith in him.

Near the end of the letter, the writer says that life is like running in a race. And all those Bible heroes of the faith have shown us how to live our lives. So we need to get rid of everything that would slow us down, like the sins or wrong things we do over and over again. We need to keep running the race God has put us in. We can do it if we keep our eyes on Jesus, for he is the one who gives us faith from the start to the finish.

We can always count on Jesus because he is the same today as he was yesterday. And he will be the same forever.

........................................................................................

Because Jesus is our High Priest, when can we talk to God?

What does the writer of the letter to the Hebrews tell us that faith is?

Name two or three Bible people who had the gift of faith.

If we keep our eyes on Jesus, how will that help us finish the race God has put us in?

........................................................................................

# John's Wonderful Vision of Heaven

REVELATION 1:9-20; 4; 14; 21-22

When Jesus' disciple John was very old, he was a prisoner on an island called Patmos. He was sent there as a punishment for preaching about Jesus.

One day as John was worshiping God, a strange and wonderful thing happened to him. He saw a vision. Even though he was wide awake, in his mind he saw Jesus in heaven. "His eyes were bright like flames of fire," John wrote. "His feet were as bright as shiny metal, and his voice made a loud sound like stormy waves against the seashore. He held seven stars in his right hand and a sword with two sharp edges in his mouth. And his face was as bright as the sun."

John fell down in front of Jesus, but Jesus put his hand on John's head and said to him, "Don't be afraid. I am the First and Last, the living one who died but is now alive forever and ever! I hold the keys of death and the grave. And I want you to write down what you see."

John saw a door standing open in heaven. The same voice spoke, sounding like a loud trumpet: "Come up here, and I will show you what must happen."

Suddenly John's spirit was in heaven, even though his body did not leave the island! "I saw a king's throne and someone sitting on it," he wrote. "Light flashed from him as from a shiny jewel, and the glow of another shiny jewel made a circle around his throne like a rainbow. Lightning and thunder came from the throne, and in front of it was a shining glass sea.

"Around the throne were four living beings. Day and night they said, 'Holy, holy, holy is the Lord God Almighty. He always was, he is now, and he always will be.'"

Then, in his vision, John heard millions of angels singing. They were gathered around the throne, praising Jesus. After that, an angel flew across the heavens, carrying the Good News about Jesus to every nation,

*In his mind, John saw a door standing open in heaven.*

tribe, language, and people. "Fear God," the angel shouted. "And praise his greatness. For the time has come when he will sit as judge. Worship him who made heaven and earth, the sea, and all the springs of water."

Then, after seeing many terrible things that will happen on earth, John saw the holy city, the new Jerusalem, coming down from God out of heaven. It was beautiful! As it came down, John heard a loud shout from the throne in heaven: "Look, the home of God is now among his people. He will live with them, and they will be his people. He will take away their tears, and there will be no more death, sadness, crying, or pain. All of that will be gone forever."

The whole city was filled with the greatness of God. It was like a shiny jewel. John said it was made of pure gold and was as clear as glass!

John heard a very important message about that city. Nothing evil will ever be done there. The only people who can go in are those whose sins have been taken away because they have asked Jesus to be their Savior. Their names are written in Jesus' Book of Life.

Jesus says, "I am coming soon!"

If we believe Jesus is the Savior, we will be happy to say with John and everyone else in God's family, "Amen! May it be so. Come, Lord Jesus!"

---

When John had a vision of heaven, how did Jesus look?

What did four living beings sing day and night around God's throne?

What are some sad things that will be taken away when we live with God in heaven?

Who will get to go to heaven?

---